Anna Webb & Jo Good

BARKING BLONDES

How two bitches taught two bitches
to survive without men

hamlyn

An Hachette UK Company
www.hachette.co.uk

First published in Great Britain in 2013 by
Hamlyn, a division of Octopus Publishing Group Ltd
Endeavour House
189 Shaftesbury Avenue
London
WC2H 8JY
www.octopusbooks.co.uk

ISBN 978-0-600-62647-3

A CIP catalogue record for this book is available from
the British Library

Printed and bound by CPI Group (UK) Ltd, Croydon CRO 4YY

2 4 6 8 10 9 7 5 3 1

Plate section: page 1 (top) © Bryan Adams; page 1 (middle)
© Paws Pet Photography; pages 2–3 © Stuart McAlister.

Editorial Director: Trevor Davies
Managing Editor: Clare Churly
Copy-editor: Marion Paull
Senior Art Editor: Juliette Norsworthy
Designer: Jeremy Tilston
Illustratior: Abigail Read
Assistant Production Manager: Lucy Carter

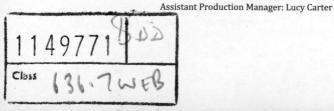

To Big George and Molly

CHAPTER 1

'We don't do bum bags.'

When I awoke that morning, I imagined I looked like a mermaid, draped on my cleverly designed glass platform bed, casting dapples of turquoise light across the room. The bed truly is a work of art, raised four foot above floor level, mezzanine style, a perfect example of how to maximize limited space.

The day dawned, however, with me looking more like a sprat wedged against two heaving bodies – three of us adrift on an ocean of snoring, grunting and blowing off, none of which came from me. I hate that side of life.

From the bed I could take in my entire bijoux Marylebone home – one room that seemed to be shrinking daily. Every surface was covered in guitars, frocks and white fur. Nobody who visited ever wore black.

Matilda, a white bulldog, shifted by the side of me, turned over on her back and continued to snore, her jowls falling to the side. The breeder had assured us that a dog, as long as it was walked, didn't need space, could live in a cupboard. Well here we were, a living demonstration of that theory.

The plan was to build her a ladder, like that scene in *West Side Story*, to assist her stubby little legs, but so far it hasn't happened and I end up carrying her, childlike, on to and off the bed. Only once has she fallen off. The noise was so loud and the vibration so strong that my downstairs neighbour came rushing up to see what had happened. Matilda didn't even flinch. She remained seated like a canine Margaret Rutherford. She weighs almost the same as I do, although we are both on restricted portions. She is on a raw tripe diet while I stick to denial. We would both like to eat more.

'Right, come on, budge. Breakfast. Matilda, move. Breakfast.'

I had managed three hours' sleep and had an 18-hour day ahead of me. It was time to get cracking. She raised one eyebrow, like a cartoon dog, squinted at me, lowered it again and carried on snoring.

Sitting up, I could see her empty food bowl, with the word BITCH emblazoned in pearls, on the floor next to a pair of massive size 10 sandals. Meanwhile, the massive size 10 feet were under the duvet, resting on her head. Big George (yes, seriously) had recently moved in, making my bed, and especially my home, feel even smaller.

When he was sitting or lying down it wasn't so bad, but once he was upright everyone and everything else turned into the Land of Lilliput. My overhead Conran lampshade was always askew from him crashing into it, and the handknitted retro pouffe remained flattened like a pancake after he sat on it. Despite many and varied attempts of mine, it had never bounced back.

Both of us loved clothes, but mine were dolly sized in comparison. All my spare quilted hangers were weighed down with loud, massive suits, leaving me with no option but to hang dresses from doorknobs.

Matilda still lay motionless, so I looked for the other option.

'George, can you let me out?' I demanded. No response. Just grunts. The only drawback to the marvellous bed is that one side is to the wall, which meant I had to climb over the two of them.

How had my beautifully organized, minimal London lifestyle become so chaotic? Here we were, three massive egos in a tiny pad and none of us willing to compromise. George had insisted, from the beginning, no dog on the bed. That rule had been broken due to our haphazard sleeping pattern. I had insisted on no cooking and no eating in, having never used my oven and never intending to. George now kept his pants in it and his headphones in the wok. As for Matilda ... well, she did what she wanted.

As much as I had fought against it, we'd become a bizarre family unit, something I'd sworn would never happen. I don't really do families. Never liked the smell of them. Family sofas and family meals panic me.

George had left his family to join my world. He had swapped one scenario for another. I hadn't asked him to. I was always adamant about that. It was his decision. If any feelings of guilt or remorse flashed through my head, he managed to convince me that they were unfounded. According to him, and from the sound of the snoring, everything was cool.

It was a filming day, which meant an early start, so I crawled over the two heaving torsos, and swung myself off the bed. Cabin fever was creeping in, but I'd allowed myself enough time to get up on the roof. I made coffee, grabbed my mug and the script and, still in pyjamas, took the pokey little lift up to the sixth floor.

I may have lived in the smallest flat in Westminster, but it was supplemented with one of the largest roof terraces on the street. Designed to be shared throughout the block, it was usually deserted since very few tenants had keys. So now it had become pretty much Matilda's recreation ground. Bits of old chews and telltale stains marked her territory.

The view was spectacular – 360° of stunning vista, including the BT Tower, London Eye and hordes of construction cranes as well as the media station where I worked. The only piece of outdoor furniture was a large, cast-iron, terracotta-tiled table, given to me by a divorced friend. It had taken six Australian removal men to carry it up the stairs. It could never be moved and had survived all types of weather. I sat cross-legged on it and sipped my coffee as I flicked through the schedule.

Morning is my favourite time of day, which is a shame because I seldom see a sunrise. For many years now, I have been the host of a late-night radio show. My working day begins when most people are getting ready for bed. For six days a week, I fall into bed at 3 a.m., and while it's great to be swimming against the tide, I miss the freshness and relative peace of an urban dawn.

Today is different: I'm up early to go filming. The television side of the radio station employs me, during the busy period, to present short documentaries. These are topical films, shot in two days with a limited crew and low budget. The days are long and exhausting even if you haven't done a radio show the night before. I'm not really a journalist, so my items are less Kate Adie and more Katie Price.

I always think television is a good idea until you do it. Radio is so much more instant and accessible. You can look like death from lack of sleep and nobody would know. On TV you pile on the slap and worry about lighting. Then everybody over-analyses the results. However, on the plus side, these films upped my profile and got my face on small screens all around the area within the confines of the M25.

Without George, I don't know what I would have done with Matilda on filming days. It would never have occurred to me to use a dog walker, partly because, being a stubborn breed, she often won't walk. I also, selfishly, dread the thought of her spending time with someone else. Luckily, George's timetable was as bizarre as mine, and Matilda was one of his top priorities. They enjoyed their days together.

A car horn tooted and I got off the table to peer over the railings. In the street below the crew truck was waiting. 'They won't be happy,' I thought. 'This feature is beneath them.' Originally, the crew had been employed as a news team, and the guys were eager to be sent on breaking stories, but today they had been assigned to me. This was to be an end-of-programme 'light' item – an 'and finally' as they are known in the trade.

'I'll be there in five minutes,' I shout down to the director.

'What's the story?' he bellows back up to the roof.

'FURKIDS,' I yell.

'What?' he yells back. 'Sperm kids?'

'No, FURKIDS,' I repeat. 'FURKIDS.'

'What they?' he demands.

The dictionary definition of furkid is 'an animal treated as a surrogate child'.

'You know why you got this job?' carped the director as I climbed into the back of the crew van. ''Cos you're known as that mad woman on the radio who goes on and on about her dog.'

He was right. This one had my name all over it. Matilda and I had acquired a reputation. As host of a daily show on local radio, I was expected to tick all the boxes and be a point of reference to whom women of indeterminate age, our target audience, could relate. But it was never the case. By my mid-forties, I'd managed to sidestep any responsibilities. No kids, so no stretch marks, no school fees, no in-laws. Just Matilda.

Yes, I had a bloke, but George was special. He understood me. Indeed, he'd been the one who had found Matilda in the first place. I think he even felt proud that he had played a part in bringing us together. If I'd had any deep down, dormant maternal instincts, I released them through my dog. But now, even George was becoming a little confused. Was he essential to my life as a lover or my dog's nanny? This question had become a recurring theme, never properly answered.

Interestingly, most of the listeners loved hearing all my dog anecdotes. And they loved George, who presented on the same station. This is why our sleep patterns were so askew. His show followed mine, so where I left off, he continued. We had become the listeners' personal little soap opera. Every detail of our daily domestic turmoil was lapped up.

It was George's idea to take Matilda for her first walk down Oxford Street. It was his suggestion to make her a toy from his massive, big-man sock. It was also his idea to buy a baby gate for the dog.

That day we had ended up queuing in John Lewis, behind Radio1 DJ Sarah Cox, who was pregnant. She looked at us with interest – either I was a granny or experiencing a phantom pregnancy. George had been right about the gate. It became a lifeline, keeping Matilda safe and giving us respite.

'Shout out the flat number,' broke in the cameraman, who doubled as van driver. 'This bloody traffic. I can't find anywhere to park.'

'Bet this is it,' I said, looking out of the window. 'Pull in behind that customized mini.'

I didn't need to check the house number. CHIEN was written on a blue and white enamel plaque on the gate. 'Very continental and chic,' I thought, and so much less aggressive than the usual BEWARE DOG. I loathe negative signage.

It was a basement flat and, in keeping with most London pads, the bins were lined up along the path towards the steps. A couple of them had had their lids knocked off and were beginning to overflow on to the ground. What looked like two hooves lay by the recycling bin. Real hooves, not the reconstituted sort you find in pet shops. They looked well chewed. Peeking out from under one of the lids and covered in coffee grounds was a pink knitted bonnet. It could have belonged to a doll or a baby except for the two slits in the sides – possibly for ears? Laden down with camera equipment as I was, I kicked the hooves out of sight and waited for the rest of the crew to catch up.

This was the Islington home of our main contributor, Anna Webb, a furkid owner who had, according to our briefing sheet, fulfilled all our criteria. The dog world is quite gossipy, but I had never heard of her, and the crew's cynicism made me more and more anxious that she would turn out to be a whiskery, fleece-clad, dog-pungent spinster. The bonnet in the bin was a worry, but the address and the 'chien' sign were positive, and I hoped there would be a connection or a shared passion for dogs. Even so, I decided it would probably be safer not to drink out of her mugs if drinks were offered. The front door was wide open and a voice drifted along from the hall ...

When we first caught sight of Anna, she was bent over, feeding meatballs to a snooty-looking dog from her bra, her long blonde hair creating a human fringe on the mutt's head. They made a comical pair as she attempted to bribe the animal to sit.

'Don't worry, they're Swedish,' she giggled, licking her dog-salivary fingers. 'Like me. Well, my mother was Swedish and I've grown up with meatballs. They make great treats.'

'Adds a whole new meaning to the expression "titbits",' commented the cameraman.

'Her roots need doing,' spat the director.

We were nearly an hour late and had dumped equipment all over her wood floor, but it didn't seem to matter, she just kept smiling. If there was an offer of coffee, I would risk her china, no problem, and, thankfully, there was no sign of a fleece.

'This is Molly,' she beamed. 'She's a miniature bull terrier and very snobby.'

Molly turned her calm, long-nosed face towards me and stared. It was like looking into a pair of human eyes from behind a dog mask. I've never gone in for cute and cosy animal patter. I no more expect spiritual connections with dogs than I do with human beings, but I honestly believe, in that moment, Molly and I understood each other. It was a look of, 'Stick with it. She's crazy but adorable. Be our friend. We understand.'

Anna's flat was a documentary maker's dream. Rock chic mixed with Rin Tin Tin. Dog memorabilia was everywhere. Door-knobs, toilet-paper holder, lampshades, cushions, rugs, mugs, paintings were all adorned with Molly's image. A cabinet was crammed with rosettes and the freezer shelves were crammed with raw tripe. Molly's three offspring, all named after rock stars, had their own portraits hanging on the living-room wall. Marley, Jarvis and Ziggy. The clues were there.

'The puppies' father was a redhead, temper and ego to match,' Anna told us. 'Lives with a mechanic now in Kent. It's more his thing; very masculine and butch in Thanet.'

Her home had everything mine lacked, including two bedrooms, corridors, space and a massive garden. Matilda would have loved it. Every floor surface was littered with chews and balls. I spied a poochie dressing-up box and even a set of flying doggles (dog goggles). Molly was obviously cherished and leading a blessed life.

'I don't do bum bags,' said Anna, offering Molly what must have been the final bit of meatball from inside her blouse. 'Always better to have the treats on you. I've found there are two types of dog people ... glamorous or smelly. I don't do smelly.'

I had my suspicions over the state of her bra by the end of the day, but otherwise I completely understood. This part-Scandinavian whirlwind certainly wasn't from the Barbara Woodhouse camp.

The by now sweaty crew began to set up for the interview. It was an amusing sight, watching them swigging tea from mugs embossed with 'Life's a Bitch', their faces grumpy. I could sense that Anna's full-on commentary was winding them up. She followed them as they plugged in cables and lights, chattering profusely. 'How about this lamp? Should I wear glasses? Should Molly wear glasses? Is that picture of Ziggy in bondage a bit over the top? Should I hide it?'

The director was getting tetchy. Molly seemed to be staring at him. I asked if maybe Molly might do a few tricks during the interview.

'Well, we could do our award-winning doggy dancing display,' Anna offered. 'It went down a storm at the Hoxton Show.'

Who wouldn't want to view this?! I asked for a little rehearsal. One blast of Little Eva's *Locomotion* from the stereo and they were off. By the first chorus, Molly, never taking her eyes off her whirling-dervish of an owner, was in her stride. She interweaved between Anna's legs, seemingly grinning as the duo culminated in a finale of gyrating legs and hip swings.

I was in heaven. This was my reward for all the dull assignments the TV channel had ever sent me on. I wanted never to leave.

Molly's outfit that day featured purple leg-warmers and has stuck fast in my mind. Here was a girl hankering for the 80s. Anna, on the other hand, was pure rock and roll – leather jacket, drainpipe jeans and designer heels. These details were important to me. A dog lover, like a busy mother, may often sacrifice fashion for practicality. But these two had style.

Anna tells me she remembers everything I was wearing, too, and that she loved my boots. They were black-patent, stiletto, over-the-knee jobs. George said they were as obvious as wearing underwear on my feet. I knew they added height and they didn't look frumpy. I have never, in my life, owned a pair of dog-walking shoes. Maybe if the two of us had dogs that actually enjoyed exercise, our footwear would be different!

Sensing Anna's ebullience and tendency to chat, I knew I had to keep the interview brief. It was just one of four segments to be slotted into a ten-minute film. The focus would be on the two of them; I would ask questions from behind the camera.

As soon as we had both been mic'd up, Anna lifted Molly on to her lap and flipped her over as you would a child. I'd never in my life seen a dog so comfortable, or so ready for an interview! Her head was on the same level as Anna's and her four legs protruded like those of an upturned coffee table.

'We travel like this on the number nineteen bus,' Anna explained. 'She enjoys being able to look out.'

Molly, uncannily, stared straight into the camera lens.

'Nuffnel in the buffnel, tuftell nood,' Anna whispered into the dog's ear.

I wasn't quite sure how to respond.

'Everything okay?' I ventured.

'Gruffall, Molly, gruffall,' muttered Anna. Molly responded with a quick lick on the nose.

Was this Swedish slang or their own secret language?

'Let's start,' muttered the director, 'and watch out for the dog's ears on that mic. It's causing a rattle.'

JO: So, Anna. Would you call Molly your baby?

ANNA: Um, she's six, so in dog years she's middle-aged, but she is the child I never had. Or indeed ever wanted. She is my soul mate.

JO: You have a very lovely home. With a strong presence of dog. Is it just the two of you living here?

ANNA: Well, there's my boyfriend, Mr Y. I named him after 'Y bother?' He edits a music magazine and is away a lot. We've been together on and off for five years. I work from home, in PR, for dog products, which is why you see so many around you.

JO: Does Mr Y see Molly as his child?

ANNA: No, he sees her as an inconvenience because she gets more of my attention than he does. I buy her fillet steak but forget to shop for him. He won't let her sleep on the bed and last night, when he was getting amorous, she appeared at the bedroom door and barked every time he moved. He issued an ultimatum that it was either him or the dog.

JO: So what happened?

ANNA: Bye bye Mr Y.

We both collapsed into laughter.

DIRECTOR: Cut!

She could have been me speaking. A hard-working, focused, childless, dog-obsessed career woman, trying to keep her partner happy and not always succeeding. As I looked around enviously at Anna's space and garden, it dawned on me that, apart from a pair of cowboy boots in the hall, there was very little evidence of Mr Y.

Her office was near the front door and next to that was the bedroom. The door was ajar and I could see Molly, fresh from her 'close-up', humping a pillow on the bed. She stopped when she heard me and looked up at the ceiling, guiltily. Mr Y certainly had his work cut out for him with this strumpet. I doubt if he ever won.

If you can never judge a book by the cover, you can always judge a person by their bookshelves. Anna's took up a whole wall. The first three volumes were biographies of musicians and I assume belonged to Mr Y. The rest were quite obviously Anna's. Every children's book ever printed about dogs was on those shelves: *The A to Z of Dogs*, *Know Your Dogs*, *Dancing With Dogs*, *The Complete Dog Care*, *Treasures of the Kennel Club*, *Illustrated Dog Watching*, *Lassie*, *Lassie Come Home*, *Greyfriars Bobby*, *Rin Tin Tin*, others in Swedish, some in French.

Anna assured me that she could guess the breed of any dog, and crossbreeds, too. Presented with the challenge, for example, of a beagle head on a pug's body, she identified a 'puggle' in an instant.

'My ambition is to go on *Mastermind* and stun the nation on the genetic combination of dog breeds,' she admitted. Unfortunately, the series has finished, so she will never have the opportunity.

A large part of Anna's childhood had been spent devouring these dog books and then being tested on the knowledge she had gained by her father. He was a retired army officer and secretary of the Shropshire branch of the RSPCA. He told Anna she would never be lonely with a dog.

'You could be in a room full of strangers and feel alone,' he said. 'But if you were in a room alone with a dog, you wouldn't feel lonely.'

Anna would accompany her dad, rattling the charity collection box, from door to door. She maintains the only bit of praise she ever got from him was for her compassion and understanding towards animals. He never suggested that eventually she would prefer dogs to people, but it was evident, from very early on, that this would be the case.

The crew had started to dismantle lights and cables and I excused myself to use the bathroom. However, once in there, I got quite a surprise. There were the usual bottles of youth-enhancing elixirs and eye-lift patches familiar to a girl about town, but the loo seat was totally unexpected. The regular one had another smaller version sitting on top of it – the sort of thing you find in children's nurseries but for an even smaller posterior and with knobbly brown bony bits set into it, making balance an impossibility. I proceeded to pee while standing on one leg.

'Oh, be careful of the loo seat,' Anna shouted through the door. 'It's a kitty latrine, meant for cats, but I'm testing it out on Molly.'

The mind boggled. If I couldn't balance on it, how was a dog or a cat going to manage? Molly may well have been clever enough to sit on Anna's lap while on the number 19 bus, but if she could achieve a poo on that contraption, she should have been in a circus!

'It's a new client,' Anna explained. 'I replaced cat litter in the seat with ground hooves. I don't usually do cats but as miniature bull terriers have cat-like feet, I reckoned Molly might clinch it. But landing with four paws on the seat at the same time is challenging even for her. I was hoping she could pee and flush by next week.'

I found the director leaning against the shed in the garden having a crafty fag.

'I'm all dogged out,' he sighed. 'Let's get the hell out. I'm covered in animal hair and I get the feeling that dog in there doesn't like me.'

'She's okay,' I cajoled. 'She's just being protective. After all, she is the only female in this joint who has given birth.'

My day of filming with Anna and Molly was the milestone you reach in life when you least expect it. In the course of my career, I have met and interviewed an endless stream of people. Some were nice and some were complete bores. When I bade farewell to most of them, it didn't bother me to think I'd never see them again. I had enough friends. I didn't need any more. Besides, many of them had reached the stage where they were dealing with kids at university or husbands with prostates. George and I didn't really fit that mould.

When people first meet Anna or me, together or separately, they often comment on how full-on and highly strung we are. And yet, from the moment I met Anna and Molly, they calmed me down. Maybe there is something to be said for like-minded souls. We are very hyper, but we understand each other's neuroses. It's a shame others can't.

I really wanted the two of them to meet Matilda. Molly, I'd been told, wasn't really interested in other dogs, but they were both bull breeds as well as bitches, so chances were they would get on.

We agreed to meet a few days later at the Honest Sausage in Regent's Park. This is the Groucho of the dog world. Situated between Primrose Hill, Marylebone and Camden Town, it attracts dogs and owners from all over central and north London. I often meet my good friend Julian Clary there with his dogs, since it's halfway between our two homes. One time we met, it all kicked off in a massive dog fight. A couple of strong-minded staffies picked on a schnauzer.

'Good Lord,' observed Julian, lighting a ciggie. 'This is turning into a sink estate!'

Usually, though, the café is calm. Bowls of water can be seen scattered around the outside tables, and there's a place to tether your dog, if you want to, a kind of 'dog park' on wheels. This contraption may often be seen taking off across the tarmac, pulled by a couple of anxious pooches with a selection of other surprised breeds tied to it.

The joy of this café, however, is its custom of selling yesterday's leftover Duchy sausages at half price, just for dogs. It's called a dog plate and is a real bargain. Many a time, George has risked it and eaten a plate of the sausages himself, or so he told me, with no disastrous results.

I parked my mini on the Inner Circle, and spotted a customized version with a union jack on the roof approaching. Anna was at the wheel. Molly, in the passenger seat, looked haughtily straight ahead. They parked in front of me and I watched as Anna, laden down with carrier bags, helped Molly out.

'Pants. Pants,' she demanded.

Molly squatted and weed on command by the side of the car. Matilda and I stared in admiration. Such bladder control and such an appropriate 'trigger' word.

The dogs, to be honest, were quite indifferent to each other. They did the usual thing of circling and sniffing and then just ignored one another. Considering how much time they were going to be together and how challenging the situations would be, we were very lucky that they got on from that first meeting.

The outing to the Honest Sausage was memorable for three things. First, Anna showed her talent for promoting doggy products, even in an outdoor café. She never appears empty handed. Whenever we meet, she will be clutching a carrier bag containing some gadget or toy or health supplement that promises to enhance the life of pet and/or owner.

We had just sat down with our plates of yesterday's bangers and mugs of coffee. We both run off coffee, the stronger the better. Cut our heads off and expresso would flood out.

'This is a Paw Plunger,' she declared, placing what looked like a toilet brush and holder on the wooden table. A family sitting with their spaniel on the next table, looked across. 'It's guaranteed to make cleaning paws less stressful. Each paw is placed, individually, into the plunger. Then wiped dry.'

She took one of Molly's paws and plunged it. Molly, obviously used to demonstrating, in any environment, waited for a few moments, removed her paw, allowed it to be dried, wolfed her dog plate, sniffed Matilda's bottom and fell asleep.

The second memorable thing still, to this day, baffles me. A middle-class, hippy type, probably from Primrose Hill, had been watching Anna's Paw Plunger antics from another table, alongside her husband. The moment she spotted Matilda snoring away, under my seat, she came over to us.

'May I look at your marvellous little bulldog?' she asked, crouching down. I nodded an agreement and carried on chatting to Anna while the woman cooed over my dog. A few minutes later she stood upright in her flowery kaftan, looked at us both and asked, 'Have you ever tried the trick of sticking your finger up her bottom?'

We were speechless.

'It makes their tongues stick out,' she added.

'As I'm sure it would ME,' snapped Anna. 'Thank you, but it's an experiment we will undoubtedly give a miss.'

If she hadn't been so posh, we'd have mistaken her for a pervert. Even now, we have no idea what was going on in her head.

The third memorable thing was that Anna first met Big George. He was never far from Matilda and me. We were always on his radar. He would have loved the three of us to spend every hour of every day together, preferably listening to the Rolling Stones. But I had been single for a long period before we met, and I still enjoyed time with my friends.

It was different for George. He had been married. He came from a background of village life, busy with work, wife, kids and recently a grandchild. He swapped all that for city madness and me. On the first night we spent together, he claimed I'd been sent by angels. He was, I thought, quite sentimental about it.

'From the moment I held your hand, my life changed,' he constantly told me, even when we had rowed. He wanted to reassure me how right we were together. According to him, I demanded nothing, no housekeeping, no chores, just good times. He was able to be himself, he insisted, and join in my metropolitan life of films, theatre, friends and fun. The more spontaneous the better. New York? Yes, let's go. So off we went, many times, and always, I'd assumed, with the full knowledge of his family.

I loved his enthusiasm for adventures and meeting my friends. The fact that we never met his, he said, was down to not having many. His size was a bonus. I've always found big man, little woman a very attractive image and was thrilled when he scooped me up and carried me home, piggyback style. It never occurred to me to ask if he was strong enough.

The crazier and busier his days, the more he enjoyed them. Maybe it was to hide from reality. Being on his own during the day unsettled him. If he awoke and found us gone, he would spend the entire day texting or calling to find us. When he had Matilda, it was okay. He would take her to all his Soho haunts and the two of them would parade the West End.

His obsession was to film or photograph everything as a record of what they had both been up to in my absence – videos of Matilda and George in Bar Italia, Matilda and George on the steps of Ronne Scott's, Matilda with the *Big Issue* seller. He was never without his camera. I seemed always to be talking into one large eye and one squinting eye behind his digital lens.

'Here comes George,' I said, sensing him lurking, paparazzi style, on the distant bandstand. 'He will love meeting you.'

We looked across the park to see a large, unmistakable figure, sporting grey ponytail, Raybans and Berkenstocks, strolling towards us. From the angle of the camera, he appeared to be filming his own approach. Matilda wriggled her bum, running towards him with excitement. Molly stood aloof.

'He has a ponytail,' Anna commented, while he was still at a safe distance.

'Yes,' I admitted.

As we stood to greet him, he filmed Matilda's reaction before laying down the camera.

'How you doin?' he grinned.

Anna tells me she initially thought, on that first meeting, that George was a bit of a prat. He was very Saint-Bernard-like in both manner and looks, she observed, but with a digital camera around his neck instead of the lovely welcoming barrel of booze.

'Anna's boyfriend writes for a music magazine,' I told George, eager to find common ground.

'Oh, then he will have heard of me,' replied George.

Now Mr Y may well have heard of Big George. His name appears at the end of *Have I Got News For You* on TV. As well as being a radio host, he had composed a number of theme tunes and that's one of them. Even so, in Anna's opinion, it was a bit presumptuous to assume he'd become a household name.

But that was George. If you hadn't heard of him, he'd make damn sure that, once you had met, you'd never forget him. He loved female company and he especially loved to see me happy. Sitting in the sunshine, he was quite happy listening to Anna and me prattling on about shoes, work and dogs.

'What's this?' he asked, holding up the abandoned Paw Plunger. 'A toilet brush?'

'Well, it's a Paw ...' began Anna.

'Oh it's just a present for me,' I interrupted.

George was not one for gadgets. Dogs, in his opinion, needed a collar and a lead. That's it. Anything else was an indulgence. I sensed Anna's products would make her ripe for teasing. It was better to head him off before it started.

'Right, girls, let's have you walking behind that tree and then laugh, wave and skip towards me,' George bellowed, seizing the digital.

'Blimey,' said Anna. 'I'm in a fashion heel. I hadn't reckoned on skipping and waving.'

Nothing would put him off.

'Jo, run, call Matilda, run, faster. Anna skip. Molly, this way.' His instructions kept coming.

'The girls at the Honest Sausage,' he spoke into the microphone, 'enjoying London sunshine.'

Later on, Anna and I were to be really grateful for these little videos. But at the time I kept thinking, 'Oh George, put the camera away. Just let's enjoy the lovely day and the walk. We don't need a record of it.' How wrong I was.

I believe only two shifts are worth doing on the radio – early morning or late at night. For four hours every night, six nights a week, George knew exactly where I would be. From 10 p.m. until 2 a.m. I was on the radio. And for a few minutes on these nights, we would be on air together, because as I signed off, he signed on. In radio jargon this is known as a 'two way'. It was also when we would reveal a little of our domestic life to the long-suffering listeners.

Many of them are London cabbies. Late-night radio, in any city, flushes out a few oddballs, but for night workers and insomniacs, overnight radio becomes a family. Our shows were mainly topical phone-ins and many callers were regulars. The saga of George and me fascinated them. After all, they had witnessed the courtship.

George, new to the station, would open his mic when he saw me walk past the studio, and sing 'My Venus in blue jeans, my whatsit in a pony tail'. On one occasion he asked for advice on how to win me over! Considering he was married at the time, it was even more brazen! Only on a 'graveyard' shift could a presenter take such risks.

'Any of you cabbies know the name of the shoes with red soles?' he bellowed one night. His voice was as large and loud and as ungroomed as he was. 'Well, I've spent the afternoon sitting on a velvet sofa, while Miss Good has stumbled up and down a store in heels so high she can't walk, that cost a bloody fortune, just so she can flash a red sole.'

'You loved it,' I butted in. 'All those flashy shop assistants offering you mineral water. It was your own private party.'

'I wouldn't mind,' he joked, 'but I always end up having to carry her home. What you need, my girl, is a pair of Crocs.'

Little glimpses, such as these, into our world kept the listeners' interest going. They loved it, and when we were out and about, cabbies would good-naturedly tease us. Matilda's arrival made the soap opera even more interesting.

'We have just brought home a bulldog puppy called Matilda,' I told them at the end of my show that night. 'We drove all the way to Hereford in George's Skoda, a family car, and she was sick in my lap on the way back.'

'Her cousin is Harry Redknapp's dog, Rosie,' butted in George. 'They share the same colouring but not the same bank account.' And he was off.

Not long after the documentary on furkids had been transmitted, Bill the cabbie, a regular caller to my show, came on the line.

'I saw you and your blonde mate in that film about women and dogs, what was it called? Fur babies or something,' he said. 'She's as barking as you are.'

'Thank you, Bill. I will take that as a compliment.'

The following night he called in again.

'Reckon your mate would know what's wrong with my staffie?' he asked. 'He's exhibiting some very antisocial behaviour.'

'I'll ask her,' I said. Then I had a thought. 'Or better still, you can.'

Next day, Anna and Molly arrived at mine with the obligatory carrier bag and a pair of mutt muffs to trial.

'These are earmuffs for dogs, to mask the sound of loud, painful noises,' she explained. 'Do you mind if we put them on the girls,' she added, stretching the pink pads over the dogs' ears, 'and walk them down Oxford Street? I'm testing them for *Your Dog* magazine, and hoping they will block out drilling and police sirens.'

As we battled against the sound of the traffic, I decided to speak to Anna about something that had been going round in my mind for sometime.

'How do you fancy doing a weekly radio show with me, about dogs?' I shouted.

Anna hardly paused to think.

'Fab, love it. Get down, Molly,' she replied. 'What shall I wear?'

My boss had once told me never to ask for permission but to ask for an apology. In other words, just do it and worry about the result later. So we didn't tell the management our plans. For the first time in its history, our radio station would be broadcasting a dog show. A station committed to breaking news would become the only radio station in the world to broadcast two whole hours for dogs and their owners, from 10 p.m. until midnight when I would carry on with my usual show. Once a week, dog items, considered to be local radio circa 1950, were going to be dragged into the 21st century, adding a sophisticated take on the canine world. And all without the bosses' consent.

So, imagine this. One Thursday at 9 p.m., two blondes and two dogs walk into the reception of one of London's most security-obsessed media hubs. I was known to the receptionists, of course, but not so Anna or the dogs. Molly was wearing doggles, not for anonymity but due to an eye infection. Matilda had on her red bow tie.

The security guards stared. We needed passes for Anna and the dogs they told us. Anna's pass was simple. I signed it. The dogs' were a bit trickier. I had no authority.

'Not even *Blue Peter* can bring pets in without a pass,' they insisted. 'The only dogs permitted in without a pass are assistance dogs.'

Looking at our two, lying flat out on the marble floor, it was obvious they couldn't really assist anyone with anything.

'They are broadcast critical,' I stated, using a term I'd heard somewhere in the newsroom. Molly yawned loudly.

'We will fill in the passes and email them to you later,' I added, full of bravado. With that, we walked past reception, holding our breath, got into the lift and pressed 'level 2 THE STUDIOS'. Phew!

At 10 p.m. that night, when usually the show would begin with a take on the day's news, Anna and I sat opposite each other, grinning, as I fired the Rolling Stones track *Walkin' the Dog*. Then we opened the mics and started.

JO: Good evening, I'm Jo Good and this is Anna Webb.

ANNA: Woof! Woof! Jo.

JO: Woof! Woof! Anna.

ANNA: Woof! Woof! Matilda.

JO: Woof! Woof! Molly. Welcome to *Barking at the Moon*. This is the only radio show in the world that dedicates two whole hours to dogs, but don't worry if you don't love dogs ... Anna?

ANNA: You'll love the people. Have you had a nice day, Molly?

Molly and Matilda, each behind a microphone, would then either grunt or bark on command. With only a sketchy running order, we soon got into our stride.

ANNA: Any pet owners out there whose mutt is suffering from post portal flatulence, I've recently discovered a cunning little gadget called 'No more Woofty from the Toofty'. Similar to a car deodorizer, it simply hangs around the dog's tail.

JO: Let's take a call from line one, Bill the Cabbie. Evening, Bill.

BILL: Woof! Woof! girls. Now, Anna ... my staffie starts to hump my wife's leg when the phone rings. What should we do?

ANNA: Woof! Woof! Bill. What you need to do is to desensitise ...

Bill had paved the way. He was followed by callers enthusing over the family pet, the trauma of losing a pet, how to cure mange. The calls kept coming. One woman in Streatham asked if we wanted to hear her boxer bark to the front door bell over the phone. We did and it barked. We then heard the neighbours banging on the wall. A *Big Issue* seller called to ask if anyone knew of a hostel that took dogs.

All the way through, Molly and Matilda slept peacefully, only joining in with enthusiastic barking when we played Perry Como's *Hot Diggety Dog*. Something they still do ...

When George came in to take over from me at the end of the show, he was as excited as we were.

'Well, how about that, folks,' he said at the top of his show. '*Barking at the Moon*. That was radio magic. This will soon become the highlight of our week.'

Four weeks into the new show, an anonymous letter was left in my locker. We were not a pen and ink office, so to see my name handwritten on a Basildon Bond envelope was a surprise.

JO AND ANNA,

JUST A WORD OF WARNING. SOMEONE HAS BROKEN OUT IN A RASH AFTER DOG HAIR WAS FOUND IN YOUR STUDIO. THERE ARE BOUND TO BE REPERCUSSIONS.

FROM

A DOG LOVER.

Well, at least we'd been warned.

'I have a wonderful device,' said Anna, 'a Suck Mutt, powerful and mighty. It sucks up dog hair and can fit into my handbag. It not only vacuums surfaces but also vacuums the dog. I can add to this a couple of reversible travel mats that the girls can sit on, preventing their posteriors ever making a connection with company carpet.'

We hoped this would buy us negotiation time. However, it was rock and roll that saved our bacon.

Deciding to plead our case, we booked an appointment with the boss. Being late-night hosts, we were seldom in the office during the day, so it was nice to be greeted by an enthusiastic workforce, as we walked confidently through the newsroom. Anna was quite a welcome sight among the rather worn-out journalists. In her drainpipe jeans and red leather jacket, with peroxided hair piled high, she drew many glances. It was nice also to hear that so many staff were fans of the show. 'Woof! Woof!' a couple of them joked. This had become our signature phrase. Admittedly, it was open to misinterpretation but generally it was meant in good humour. All I could think, however, walking past the desks, was that somebody here was a sneak who had run sneezing to management.

The boss wasn't quite so enthusiastic to see us. It was the day of local elections and all his energy was focused on sorting out staffing rotas. Decisions about dogs in studios was not a priority and it was evident from his manner that the Suck Mutt wasn't going to swing it.

'Not even Jenni Murray's chihuahas are permitted in the *Woman's Hour* office,' he insisted.

'Maybe not, but our dogs are integral to the show,' I countered. 'The only way we manage to get the A list guests to come into the studio is because they love being on the radio talking about their dogs in the presence of our dogs. We never invite them to bring their own pets as that would be too risky.'

The boss stared out of the window at his busy workforce, I wondered if he was wishing we would both disappear.

'We could bring them in through the side door, sit them on mats, vacuum the fur up at the end of the show and avoid contact with any other work space,' I suggested.

He continued to avoid eye contact. His silence seemed to herald the day of our demise.

'Bryan Adams is coming on the show this week,' interrupted Anna. 'We promised him that Molly could sit on his lap and join in a chorus of *Everything I Do*. He will cancel coming in if she isn't in the studio.'

The boss swung round. 'THE Bryan Adams?' His expression had changed. He was positively beaming. 'I proposed to my wife during his rendition of *Thought I'd Died and Gone to Heaven*. Any chance you could get him to sign my CD?'

Job done. The show, along with the dogs, was safe. At least until the next time.

Anna's dog-loving, ex-army dad had been Bryan Adams' godfather, and he hadn't passed on just his love for dogs but also a lust for heavy rock. Anna was strongly attracted to rock stars. She saw herself as a bit of a latter-day Paula Yates. On nights when she wasn't working, she and Y Bother could often be found at a gig, grooving on down with the kids. Mr Y enjoyed the status of taking an attractive blonde with a bull terrier to his work assignments. As he grabbed interviews with various personalities, he would leave the girls in the VIP enclosure, where they became a familiar sight, mingling with musicians and their entourage. Molly in her pink muff mutts could easily give Gwyneth's and Chris from Coldplay's baby Apple a run for her money.

Saturdays and Sundays, however, were exempt. Anna's and Molly's diary dictated that gigging with live bands could happen only in the week. Weekends were exclusively dog days, and they were packed. There was dog camp, doggy dancing, obedience and agility. They didn't socialize at these events. As Anna says, she doesn't do bum bags.

Anna would drive to a local dog show, enter Molly for a partic- ular class, win a rosette and then drive straight home. The rosette would be squashed into the already overflowing cabinet and they would both celebrate with an evening in. Molly's Saturday night meal would be lovingly prepared to include raw tripe, blueberries, natural yoghurt and royal jelly. Anna would settle for a glass of pinot grigio and a Marlborough.

In the early hours, exhausted and with his ears still ringing, Mr Y would often arrive home to find them asleep in bed, Molly's head on his pillow. Frustrated at not being able to talk about the evening, he would prod Molly in an attempt to wake her.

One night, after a particularly lacklustre interview, he arrived back in need of affection and shoved the sleeping Molly on to the floor. She bit him on the arm. This woke Anna, who threw a pillow and a hissy fit, pushed Mr Y into the living room and told him to sleep on the sofa. Not the homecoming he had desired.

'He's a fair-weather dog lover,' Anna told me. 'He shows Molly off to all his cool friends when it suits him, but when it comes to celebrating her achievements, he doesn't want to know. I'm constantly having to step between them.'

I suspected Mr Y had other thoughts on his mind during these late nights, and they wouldn't be Molly's rosettes.

Thursday nights were now another date in Anna's diary, another night that kept her and Mr Y apart. *Barking at the Moon* was becoming very popular and very time consuming. We were spending more and more time devising entertaining and original running orders. We no longer had to beg celebrities to turn out in the middle of the night. They started queuing up in anticipation. The dog world is a bit like the Mafia; word spread and some kudos appeared to be attached to coming on our show.

Listeners began sending in obscure dog tracks to be played throughout the show. We struck gold, however, when the Jive Aces, who later reached the semi-finals of *Britain's Got Talent*, offered to be our house band. They composed the show's eccentric theme tune and arrived on Thursdays decked out in their signature bright yellow suits. Thank heavens for mutt muffs on those nights with a full band in the studio.

We treated Thursdays like a theatrical event. Anna would always call me prior to setting off for the studio.

'What are you wearing tonight?'

It didn't matter that we were on the radio – there was a studio webcam and we liked to make use of it. We don't do 'casual'.

'My clogs and my Ben de Lisi French bulldog T-shirt.'

'Right, good. I'll wear the same. Mr Y is going to have to run us there. My mini has a flat tyre,' she told me one night.

It was odd to hear Anna in need of a favour. The two of us are fiercely independent and we always manage to get ourselves out of scrapes with little or no help from anyone. However, Y Bother was on his way to a gig at the 100 Club off Oxford Street, so he could give them a lift in and pick them up on the way back. His car drew up outside the radio station at the same time as mine, Mr Y driving, Anna in the passenger seat, looking straight ahead, Molly on her lap. If you had pulled up beside them at traffic lights, they would have made you smile. I'd met Mr Y a couple of times before and he was good fun, if a little intense.

'Quite the little family,' I laughed, helping the girls to get out of the car.

'She's dribbled on my cashmere,' he muttered, dabbing dog hairs off his sleeve.

'Woof! Woof! Girls,' a passing London cabbie shouted out of his window.

'Jesus,' said Mr Y. 'Why do they do that? It's so misogynistic.'

'It's funny,' said Anna. 'Lighten up. Have a good time at the gig.'

'You could both come with me,' he said. 'It's Imelda May's last gig before the tour. Could easily get you in.'

'We have a crucial demonstration with a police sniffer dog to sort for tonight's show,' responded Anna. 'I told you, Thursday nights are impossible. But you have fun. Enjoy Imelda and don't forget to pick me up back here at midnight.'

Y Bother drove off in a huff just as an old battered transit van drew up. We stood and watched as our two guests for the night emerged. They were ex-police-dog trainer Terry and his dog Boycie. We watched with respect. The dog never took his eyes off his master but simply walked by his side, waiting for commands. Terry didn't say a word. Just nodded at us.

If the security guards in reception were initially a bit taken aback by Molly and Matilda in the early days, they simply stood aside to let these two through.

Terry had retired from the police force the previous year, along with his earnest and hard-working black labrador, Boycie. However, they still had the smell of the forces about them. They had become experts in searching for explosives and had acquired a reputation as a remarkable team, even working for the Queen. Now they travelled the country, demonstrating a dog's ability to find through scent. This was to be their first time in a radio station.

We immediately noticed their economy in, well, everything – speech, behaviour, enthusiasm. Nothing seemed to change their tempo. It was all very understated. While Anna and I are prepared to admit that we operate on full throttle, these two never appeared to get out of first gear.

Alone in the green room, Boycie, unlike most dogs new to an environment, didn't attempt to sniff about; he simply lay by his master's feet. Terry, holding a folder full of yellowing press cuttings, sat just as patiently, waiting to be given his instructions.

Anna, concerned that Molly might take against Boycie due to 'having history' with a labrador, took it upon herself to act as hostess.

'Now, I'm going to do a little desensitising exercise,' she announced to the guests. 'Boycie, this is Molly. Nufftall grafull, Molls. And this is Matilda. Gruffall in the beebal, be nice everybody.'

She had launched into her dog language in front of a retired police officer and his disinterested hound. Leading our two dogs, both dressed in matching pink bandanas that evening, in circles around our two guests, she chatted away nervously. I began to panic.

Terry continued to sit and say nothing while Anna took on the role of cocktail socialite.

'I have something tucked in here that Boycie might enjoy,' Anna said, reaching into her bra for a warm meatball. I thought I saw a flicker in Terry's eye.

'No food,' he said quietly.

'Ah yes, of course,' said Anna as she self-consciously popped it into her own mouth.

I couldn't quite work out how this pair's talent was going to translate on radio. Terry wasn't at all verbose, and getting Boycie to bark along to Elvis's *Hound Dog* didn't seem appropriate.

'Terry, the moment we start the show I think it's best we have your search and discover demonstration and finish with a quick interview. Does that sound okay?'

Terry nodded. 'I've brought our training bag,' and he gestured to a haversack lying on the floor.

'Fab,' Anna and I said in unison.

Maybe he will warm up a little when we get on air, we thought, when Dr Footlights kicks in. We left him for a few minutes and started to prepare the studio.

Looking back, it was inevitable that a dog show on the radio would hit a few hitches. But we had grown bold. Conquering the rule about no dogs in the building, we had become giddy with our growing success and convinced we had won over the management.

The night of the police sniffer dog demonstration, as it became known, started like any other show with Molly's and

Matilda's familiar singing and snoring antics. Then we introduced our guests.

ANNA: As London is on high alert, heading towards the 2012 Olympics, security is obviously being toughened up.

JO: Police sniffer dogs are going to be working to their full ability as they help Londoners keep moving. Tonight, joining us in the studio, we have a highly respected pair. Retired police-dog trainer Terry and his talented, trusted friend, Boycie.

ANNA: 'Woof! Woof! Terry

Silence.

JO: Welcome to *Barking at the Moon*, Terry. Woof! Woof!

Silence. Then Matilda snored.

This was our signature phrase. Most guests loved it. Not this one.

JO AND ANNA: Come on, Terry! Woof! Woof!

TERRY: Evenin'.

JO: Now, Terry, we are all in for a treat tonight as you and Boycie have agreed to a demonstration for the listeners. This will reveal just how acute a dog's sense of smell is, and how it can be used in a possible terrorist situation. If you would like to move closer to the mic, Terry, perhaps you could take us through it step by step.

Terry, now becoming a little more animated, stood up and looked down at Boycie.

ANNA: Ah, I see you want to demonstrate standing up, so I'm going to follow you with my hand-held mic.

TERRY: (talking into Anna's mic): I took it upon myself to plant Boycie's training bag somewhere in the building. When I give him the command, I would like you to open this studio door. Boycie will find the bag, stand by the side of it and bark until I join him. He must not retrieve it and bring it back to me, obviously.

JO: Obviously. How exciting. I hope all of you at home realize how lucky we are to have an empty newsroom so that we can take this opportunity to stage this exciting demonstration.

ANNA: I will be following Boycie with my hand-held mic so that I can describe just how he goes about this task.

JO: Very well, Terry. In your own time.

Terry clicked his fingers, opened the studio door, and Boycie sprung to his feet.

TERRY: (quietly): Seek.

Boycie, on a mission, headed straight into the newsroom with Anna, clutching her hand-held mic, following.

ANNA: Well, he's had a quick sniff round Vanessa Feltz's desk, he's now heading towards the lockers ... sniffing up and down, pausing and, again, sniffing.

JO: (still in the studio): I suppose, Terry, the training bag has an attractive smell in it that must be encouraging him to hunt?

TERRY: Yes, it's soaked in Semtex. We can't smell it but Boycie certainly can.

The world stood still. I saw our careers, along with the entire building, crashing to the ground. Not even Anna, who is great in a crisis, could rescue this one. The producer had slumped in his chair. Only Boycie was moving. Then he stopped. And barked.

ANNA: (croaking): He, um, he seems to be by the side of Danny Baker's locker ... Oh Lord.

I couldn't speak. I just sat there as Terry walked into the newsroom, retrieved Boycie and the bag and came back into the studio. Matilda was still snoring.

'He's carrying explosives!' my producer's voice screamed through my headphones. 'Get him out!'

JO: Well, there we must leave it. Terry, Boycie, we must crack on with the show. Lovely to see you both at work, safe journey home. Let's have a tune now from the Monkees.

If our show had nine lives, it was losing them rapidly. The producer had attempted to hang his sweater over all the webcams to prevent footage of the Semtex-soaked bag being shown. We waited for the phones to ring but, strangely, the only reaction we had came from a lady in Norwood, who demanded to know why Terry hadn't said 'Woof! Woof!' before he left.

The next morning I was up on the roof with Matilda, counting cranes, when my phone rang. Dreading answering it, in case it was the boss, I let it go to voicemail. Thirty-four cranes I noted across the skyline, the most I had ever seen. We must be heading out of the recession. My dad had been in the building industry and I've inherited his fascination with construction and destruction. George was the same. Many of his thousands of photographs taken on daily walks depicted the speed at which this city creates and destroys architecture. We had walked around many urban building sites. Matilda has peed on many a foundation. I listened to my voicemail. It was Anna.

'Molly! Get down! Oh Christ, Jo, I'm losing the plot. Y Bother is a shit! A complete shit! You know he didn't pick me up last night. Well, he came back drunk, disturbed me and Molls and was then sick over her embossed cashmere blanket. Molly hasn't stopped shaking. She won't eat her tripe and is biting her toes. I'm coming over. Just need to chill on your roof.'

Anna's voicemails were often a complete scenario – a beginning, a middle and an end. Molly, as always, appeared in every chapter.

I made a huge pot of coffee and waited for their arrival. It was strange that George wasn't around. Usually, by now, he had taken at least 20 snaps of us in various stages of 'habille'. I guessed he was in town, maybe at his composer's forum.

I threw my house key down into the street for Anna to let herself in when I spotted the familiar Union Jack mini draw up.

'Woof! Woof!' shouted a passing cabbie. She didn't seem to want to answer.

Knowing she wouldn't take the lift because exercise was good for Molly, I waited for their breathless arrival on the roof. Matilda was there before me, and charged towards the terrace door.

'Molls, Molls, Molls,' I shouted, hoping she would do her party piece of pirouettes and leaps. I'm afraid I always greet her like this. Any dog trainer will tell you it's wrong but she never lets me down. There was a wonderful crescendo of barking from both dogs, excited to see one another. Anna appeared close behind, out of breath and laden down with what looked like brightly coloured sex toys.

'Here girls, fetch.' She threw them across the terrace. 'It's a new contract. Doggy Dreams. They're rubber, indestructible, and I know they look pornographic but Molly loves them.'

So did Matilda. As we downed mugs of coffee, both dogs, brandishing what resembled dildos, ran up and down around us. Molly was still wearing her lead. The roof terrace has railings all the way around it apart from a small section far away at the very end. From that point, it was a sheer drop to the pavement below. This never worried me because Matilda was not the sort of dog that would bolt, and she never ventured very far across the roof. Occasionally, I would even leave her up there to soak in some fresh London air while I was cleaning the flat. She would always remain right where I'd left her.

Anna, on the other hand, was manic about the gap in the railings and with some justification. Molly, being a terrier, would sometimes just take off. No amount of calling would get her back until she felt like it. This happened in parks or in the country, wherever she was let off the lead. I secretly thought she did it to play Anna up, and the screaming and hollering to get her to come back was often embarrassing.

It was one of Anna's foibles constantly to watch out for imminent, Molly-life-threatening situations. I never questioned it even though I could see how others around reacted. She loved Molly so much that any thought of a life without her was impossible. To some, this verged on the macabre, but the more time I spent with them, the more I noticed an invisible umbilical cord.

'He doesn't get it.' Anna launched straight in with her frustration over Y Bother. 'That blanket was a gift from a client. It came from Harrods' pet department. His drinking is boring. So is his obsession with sex. I had just gone through the stress of a stranger introducing explosives into a major broadcasting building. I was exhausted. The last thing I wanted was leg over. Molly, get down.'

'Maybe he feels left out,' I offered, sensing a familiar scenario.

'I can't be blamed for his insecurity,' she continued. 'It's as though he's jealous of my dog. I catch them sometimes just staring at each other. With loathing. Molly always outstares him. He gets his revenge by pretending to forget to let her in when she goes out for a pee. At night they both race to be the first to get their head on the pillow. It's ridiculous. Mind you, Molly always wins.'

I was beginning to feel quite sorry for the chap.

'Why is it I can quite happily pick up Molly's poo but I refuse to pick up his Y fronts?' she asked.

I was stumped by this one. Fortunately, my mobile started ringing. It was George.

'I can see you,' he said.

'You can't,' I replied. 'I'm up on the roof.'

'I know, I'm watching you. You're wearing green jeans, white top, and the dogs look like they're playing with sex toys.'

I started turning round. Where was he? The roof couldn't be overlooked from any other block.

'Guess where I am,' he goaded. I could hear the childlike excitement in his voice. 'Look up.'

I looked up at the sky. Surely he wasn't crazy enough to be in a helicopter.

'I'm in the BT tower,' he laughed. 'Right at the top, where the revolving restaurant used to be. I've got the security guy's binoculars. It's amazing. I've taken ariel shots for you of every crane in a five-mile radius. The biggest one is the one over the Langham Hotel. It's got a mobile toilet for the crane driver half-way down.'

His enthusiasm was infectious. I wished he'd taken me with him. Up in the sky, counting cranes.

'Wave,' he shouted. 'All of you wave so I can get a picture.'

I grabbed Anna and together we held the dogs, who, sensing our excitement, had started jumping up and down.

'We're waving,' we yelled. 'Hello! We're waving and the dogs are barking!'

'Move more to the left, get rid of those mugs, push the chairs to the side.' Even at the top of a tower he was issuing posing instructions. 'Now smile, come on, big smiles. Right. I've got a few good ones there. See you later.'

We will never know how he bluffed his way into the tower but the phone call had raised our spirits.

'I'm going to make us more coffee,' I said to Anna. 'We need to think of what to put in next week's running order. Keep an eye on Matilda.'

I went downstairs to my flat smiling at the thought of George, Saint Bernard like, as Anna described him, plodding his way back, with a camera full of aerial views. He actually 'got' me – cranes, dogs, shoes, the lot. Unlike Mr Y, George had obviously embraced the theory 'if you can't beat 'em, join 'em'.

On the kitchen shelf he'd left me a packet of microwave popcorn. I live off the stuff – few calories and it doesn't require cooking, but it's not easy to find. George bought it for me whenever he did a shop. Along with not cooking, I don't food shop. Anna, also forever on a diet, loved popcorn. Thinking we had a couple of hours of graft ahead of us, I heated some in a bowl to take up.

When I emerged back on the roof with popcorn and a fresh pot of coffee, I found Anna sitting with a massive grin on her face.

'Oh my God!' she said. 'Oh my God!'

'What?' I asked.

'Oh my God! You won't believe what's happened. You won't believe who has just called us.'

'Who?' I yelled. I'd only been gone a few minutes. The call was obviously more exciting than a new contract for puppy pads.

'Pulse Films. Hannah, the director of Pulse Films.'

'Who are Pulse Films? Tell me, please tell me,' my voice was rising in tandem with her excitement.

Anna, taking her time, whether for dramatic effect or because she was still trying to absorb it all, stood up to deliver the next bit.

'It's the production company who made *The Pineapple Dance* reality television show. Apparently, they're about to start a new series on, wait for it, dogs and their owners. This girl Hannah says she was shown the videos of us with the girls that George had put online. She wants to know if we are available to be in all twelve episodes.'

I stood holding the coffee pot, dazed.

'She said she will call back in a minute. They need to know today so they can sort a schedule. There's an item on a bulldog picnic in Bognor this weekend and they need to know if we can get there. I said you were just downstairs. We can do it, can't we? We'll just have to fit everything else around it. Can't we?'

I was nodding and grinning at the same time. Anna's phone rang. It was Pulse Films.

'Yes, I've spoken to Jo, yes we would love to. I'll hand her over ...' she began.

My phone started to ring. It was George.

'Hello,' I snapped.

'I'm in a crane!' he yelled. 'I'm in the tallest crane. Look up and you'll see me.'

'Oh George,' I said. 'Not now. Tell me later. We're on the phone to a production company.'

He hung up.

CHAPTER 2

'We felt as vital as a pair of young Bardots.'

I love Selfridges. They have a dog policy. Pick them up and they're permitted. Dogs are allowed to shop, but only if they are carried. That's great if you have an 'air dog' (one that can be held above ground or placed in a handbag), such as a chihuahua or a yorkie, but try carrying a bulldog for any length of time.

Big George with his big arms managed brilliantly. He was a geezer. Dressed in his long black cashmere coat, he would lift up Matilda as a puppy, hold her plump little white body under his arm and strut proudly through the store. As he passed their counters, shop assistants would follow him, Pied-Piper-like, desperate to have a look at the baby bulldog carried by the big man with the pony tail.

His favourite counter was Jo Malone. He would spray the two of them in grapefruit cologne, or any tester thrust at him by a member of staff, and then stand like a proud father among the shop girls, who were grateful for any distraction. I remember looking at all the admirers and thinking this must be what it's like wheeling around a newborn baby – except in this instance, the surrogates were knocking on a bit and the offspring had a wicked underbite.

As Matilda matured, her weight became quite a challenge, but George with his mighty arms strutted more flamboyantly. The three of us became a familiar sight. It was, after all, our corner shop.

On this day, we were heading for the luggage department in the basement, which meant an escalator ride. Holding the heavy Matilda under one arm, George started drumming out the rhythm of what sounded like *Black Betty* on the handrail with the fingers of the other hand. I never knew if his drumming was a habit or an effort to draw attention to his musician status.

As we descended, the sight of a hefty-looking bulldog held by a bloke drumming out rock and roll made shoppers on the up journey burst out laughing.

'Man, I could do with a spray of citrus,' George said as we walked towards some suitcases. 'This going to take long?'

An assistant with a name tag – 'Amanda Luggage Liaison' – spotted us and looked ready to pounce.

'I need a small hand-luggage case on wheels,' I replied. 'It won't take long. Please stop drumming.'

I started to busy myself with suitcases, trying them out and lifting them up, while George placed Matilda on the ground. She lay on the marble in her frog pose and Amanda Luggage Liaison admired her profile.

We were hidden behind a display of massive trunks but still attracting attention from an eagle-eyed, supervisory, spotting-type person. Could this person see Matilda sprawled on the floor?

'I'll take this one,' I said, wheeling a discreet-looking designer case in patent leather. George picked up Matilda and we followed Amanda Luggage Liaison towards the till.

'Where will you be travelling to?' she asked.

'New York,' responded George.

'Paris,' said I at the same time.

We turned slowly to look at each other, a bit like in a Woody Allen film.

'What?' said George. 'Paris? Bleedin' heck. Are we going to Paris? I thought we were going to New York. We agreed we would follow up our contacts in Manhattan. Prepare ourselves for the big shift. Jeez, we can't afford to ponce off to Paris.'

Amanda Luggage Liaison looked embarrassed.

'Not this time,' I said. 'This time it's Paris with the dogs and Anna.'

New York meant everything to George and me. It was where we had the most fun, and we were pretentious enough to call it our spiritual home. When finances were good and we risked taking time away from the radio shows, we would head straight for the Big Apple. Like all old rockers, we stayed at the Chelsea Hotel and George would tell me tales of past residents. Occasionally, we might see Dylan, or someone who looked like him, sitting in reception. Every guest had a story and we convinced ourselves we fitted right in.

Next door to the Chelsea was a guitar shop. I would leave George there to play while I had my toes pedicured in the salon across the road.

We walked everywhere, including from the Dakota Building all the way through to Harlem and the infamous Apollo Music Hall. On that day, we walked into the centre of Harlem, noticed the mood change and began to get a bit twitchy. George's bravado seemed to shrink as a group of kids spotted us from a street corner. One of them pointed, nodded back in the direction of Central Park and said, 'Hey, white people, you going the wrong way.'

We didn't blame them. They must have seen two middle-aged hippy types treating their neighbourhood like an adventure park. But it made us smile and George went over to the kid and said, 'Man, I like your style.' The kids laughed and they all high-fived.

George was at his happiest when we were abroad and he had me all to himself with no distractions. He would go up to anybody with his camera, and say, 'Do you mind, mate?' He'd grab me by putting one massive arm around my waist and we would be snapped in what was always quite an unnatural pose. He did this everywhere we went, as though he wanted a record of every minute. Most importantly, it was in New York's Union Square that we fell in love, at first sight, with a white bulldog.

We'd stopped to eat lunch, sitting on the grass, and an elderly guy in leather bondage gear sat beside us, talking on his phone. By his side was a bulldog. Ignored by her owner, she lay on her back, all four legs in the air, jowls flapping apart, and wriggled. As soon as she smelt our food she flipped herself upright, trotted over and sprawled in a starfish-style pose at our feet.

Dressed, like her owner, in a leather harness, she stared up at us, waiting for scraps. The guy finished his call, stood up, brushed himself down and started to walk off, which was when we noticed that he was wearing leather chaps with the bottom cut out. His dog followed him immediately. The sight of both of their bottoms wiggling away from us, one bare and the other covered in white fur, was bliss. 'That's the dog for us,' we thought.

New York was also our Plan B. When the broadcasting world spat us out, and our treasured BBC passes ceased to work, then Manhattan's East Village would surely welcome us into its rock-and-roll village life.

The plan was to get straight on a plane and begin a new life in the Big Apple. Details like having no visa, no apartment and no job prospects didn't deter us. I knew a producer at a satellite radio station. Neil. That was enough. We would live off love and help from Neil. Looking back, how on earth did we ever think we would survive? George, forever the optimist, insisted he would get work by writing for music magazines. I believed him. The only positive bit of preparation we had made for New York and Plan B was Matilda's pet passport – George had taken a lovely head and shoulders shot of her – and because it could take ages to organize from this side, we had kept it up to date, ready for our quick getaway.

I looked now at his disappointed face.

'It's only for the weekend,' I said. 'Come on, George. I agreed I'd drive the three of us and Anna and Molly to Paris through the tunnel. It has to be next weekend because the screen test for the TV series is the following week, and if we pass, this will be the last opportunity we have for a break all summer.'

I hadn't kept him up to date with all the discussions. Nothing had yet been finalized over the reality series and Anna and I could have been accused of naïve optimism. However, calls from the production office revolved not only around the screen test, but also our availability until autumn. If they decided to use us, we would be filming every weekend, and these couple of days in Paris would be our only summer holiday.

George tenderly put Matilda back down on the floor, near a kitchen display of saucepans. This was an obvious health and safety risk and a bit like waving a red rag to a bull in front of the supervisory, spotting-type person.

'Look, man, I'm not travelling in a tiny mini to Paris with your mate and two dogs,' he said. 'Specially with you driving on the right-hand side of the road. It's bad enough on the A3.'

'Anna will be driving on the French side,' I said, watching the supervisory, spotting-type woman clock Matilda and start to walk towards us. 'She's lived in France and can do hand signals,' I added.

'Forget it,' he continued. 'I'm not sitting in a tiny car with my knees round my neck all the way to Paris and you bossing us, man. You know what I think of Anna. She's a great chick but she's bonkers.'

Supervisory, spotting-type woman had reached us.

'Sir, would you mind picking your dog back up?' she asked nicely. Matilda had managed to get her head into a saucepan.

'Sure, mate.' George lifted her up; then, over his shoulder, he said to me, 'Count me out. I've got tunes to write.'

Quel dommage!

Anna considers herself to be quite Parisienne. I'm always impressed by her skill with scarves, almost pure haute couture. When she was in her 20s, she lived in Paris, working for a sound magazine, near Notre Dame. Her apartment was in the 4th Arrondisement, in the Marais, the equivalent of London's Soho. She adored the city, the language, its architecture, style and, of course, love of dogs.

Always with an eye for breed spotting, she noticed how the French favoured pure breeds rather than mongrels. If the owners were chic, so were their pooches, and especially the well-coiffed poodles. Even 20 years ago, according to Anna, Parisians welcomed dogs into café society while London still struggles not to discriminate.

'I would sit in the Jardin Etoiles most lunch hours,' Anna told me, 'and identify breeds and their fashionable owners. I promised myself that one day I would revisit with a dog of my own.'

Part of me was amazed that a pretty 20 something blonde would spend her leisure hours in the 'city for lovers' ogling poodles. While many found the breed absurd, Anna admired their style and intelligence.

Her year in Paris, she admitted, was far from well behaved. She lived among a decadent, stylish and hedonistic musician community and partied along with all of them. But always in her mind she knew it would have been so much better with a dog. Now, 20 years on, she was taking Molly .

'I've wanted to take Molls through the Eurotunnel for years,' she told me. 'I'm eager to show her my Paris, practise my French and walk us down Montmartre in the moonlight. I want us to sit at the grave of Rin Tin Tin. He's buried in a cemetery that's just for dogs.'

This was said with as much enthusiasm as any parent keen to introduce their offspring to a land and a chapter from their past. Molly was going to be shown another country through Anna's eyes. Everything Anna saw and experienced was relevant only if Molly was by her side. She believed that to keep her dog alert, Molly needed as much mental stimulation and experiences as any child.

'I'm viewing this trip for the girls as educational,' she told me as we packed the boot of my mini. 'No language problems because they speak the universal language of dog, and think of all the stimulation and new smells of a springtime in Paris.'

I imagined Y Bother would also have enjoyed springtime in Paris, but there was no mention of him. Had he, like George, admitted that a trip across the Channel in a small car with two dogs would be his kind of living hell?

George and I had visited Paris the previous year and had an enjoyable but touristy time, ending with him photographing me on every level of the Eiffel Tower. So I felt less guilty about him staying behind. I tried to convince myself that he would enjoy spending a couple of days in my tiny flat, just hanging out in London. Knowing how he loved to sit strumming his guitar on the bed for hours, I'd hidden a half bottle of his beloved brandy under the duvet. This was his idea of a good night in.

For me, the trip would be the first time abroad with Matilda. It would have been more fun if George had agreed to come with us but, even so, we would be in the company of her now best friend Molly. Led by Anna, an ex-resident who spoke fluent French, we would be shown a Paris I had never before seen.

We had decided to travel in my mini because, although it wasn't as groovy as Anna's customized version, it was newer and covered by Relay.

'Best we travel light,' said Anna, 'in case we want to do some shopping over there. I've left half the boot available for the girls' cases.'

Anna considered her dog's health and comfort very seriously. Molly's luggage took up most of the dogs' half of the boot. There was an attaché case solely for diet and health. In it there must have been up to 20 different supplements, ranging from fresh royal jelly to zinc, acidophilus and Chinese herbs; two rolls of bandages; and a carton of paw plasters. Then there was a sack of calves' hooves for chewing in the hotel, bottled water and endless plastic cartons of frozen (and now thawing) green tripe placed in cooler bags. Molly's cashmere blanket, toys and wardrobe, including a life jacket, were in a separate case. Anna's own bag was modest by comparison.

I looked, with a sense of guilt, at my new suitcase, bursting with my favourite clothes and make-up. But far worse was the meagreness of Matilda's luggage. I placed a Sainsbury's bag containing four tins of dog food next to Molly's pile of cases. That was it. Matilda had become the kid sent off on the school trip with spam sandwiches.

'Right,' said Anna as we set off. 'I've used all my contacts and I've managed to get us quite a good deal.' I looked suitably impressed. 'It took a while to sort but I've managed to swing it so that there is a designated toilet area for the dogs either end of the tunnel, and we each get a complimentary cheese roll ... on the outward and inward journey.' Luxury indeed.

Both our dogs are lazy and love car journeys. Forget the theory that all dogs need to run free – our two prefer the fastest possible route, with the least amount of effort. Heading towards Folkestone, strapped in on the back seat, each looking out of the window, they appreciated the passing countryside, and that was all the exercise they wanted.

We had agreed that, once through the tunnel, Anna would take over, since she had some knowledge of France and had driven on the right. Until then, I was behind the wheel.

Going through the designated customs for passengers with pet passports, we both got very excited. Neither of us had travelled with dogs before, and knowing how attractive and well behaved they looked, we bathed in the looks of approval from the staff. We had given a great deal of thought to their passport photographs. George's snap of Matilda was in profile and she was wearing her red bow-tie collar; Anna had photoshopped Molly so that she looked younger than her eight years, but it was still a good likeness.

'Maintenant nous parlons français seulement,' proclaimed Anna.

'What?' I answered.

'We now speak only French,' she replied. 'Even to the dogs. It will be testing for them.'

'Au contraire, it will be testing for me,' I said. 'I have a failed French O-level.'

We were still in Folkestone, on the train, sitting in the car with the windows open, waiting patiently to depart, when the dogs started to pant. At the same time Anna's smart phone started bleeping with incoming texts.

'Who's that texting?' I asked. 'Is it Y Bother?'

'No, no this is important,' Anna replied. 'The pet barometer on Molly's collar is linked to my phone and it's telling me her temperature is sky high. I'm getting out to grab the Fido in Flight travel flask from the boot.'

Thank heavens she was speaking English. It seemed to be allowed in an emergency.

Anna had only just opened her door when a brusque French-accented male voice seemed to float in from up above.

'Ah Madame, plees would you kindly stay in your car until we start to move.'

A smartly uniformed French Eurotunnel official was pushed against our bonnet. He was dressed like a soldier in an opening scene from an opera. No high-viz gear on this workforce. Très chic.

'Pardon Monsieur,' replied Anna. 'C'est nos chiens qui avez soif. Je vais les emporter d'eau. Pardon Monsieur.'

'Merci Madame,' he responded, and then, in perfect English, 'but if you need water for the dogs, you must sit, like them, and be good, yes? No wagging the tails until we move.'

We looked at each other and giggled. What fun this trip was proving to be.

'I've forgotten to call George to say we're about to go through the tunnel,' I suddenly realized. 'I promised I'd let him know when we got here.'

The train lurched and started to move.

'Too late now,' said Anna. 'I'll text Y Bother when we get to Calais. We won't get a signal in here anyway. Right, girls, let's keep our spirits up, as Miss Stamp my zoology teacher used to say, and sing a song. I know, the noodle, doodle song.'

The noodle, doodle song is Anna's made-up travelling song for Molly. It's to stop boredom on long journeys. Probably Anna's own boredom, because our dogs have no capacity for boredom. They are lazy.

The lyrics are, to be honest, quite embarrassing in their childishness, but then it was never intended to be overheard. Sung to the tune of a familiar nursery rhyme, it is, apparently, a celebratory anthem they both indulge in after a rosette win on the journey home – Molly has learned to bark spontaneously during the chorus. I'd been privy to it on one previous occasion when we had been stuck in traffic on the Euston Road. It sent me into fits of laughter and Anna sheepishly admitted that it was the only time anyone else had heard it. Whizzing through the tunnel, the girls still strapped in on the back seat, where better to practise a round.

'A commencez, mes petites,' said Anna to the puzzled duo. 'Chansons loud et clear.'

'Noodle in your pants, noodle in your pants, merrily, merrily, merrily, merrily, noodle in your pants,' we sang out, and Molly, always sensitive to a celebratory atmosphere, joined in with spectacular barking. Our car was in a long line with others, all with their windows only half open and their air conditioning on, so we reckoned we were safe from disrupting fellow travellers. We decided to go for a second chorus.

'Noodle in your pants ...'

'Pardon Mesdames,' the voice of the Tunnel man cut in as he appeared from behind our car and leaned his head in through my window.

We stopped singing and Molly lay down and hid her face self-consciously in the back of her seat. Her embarrassment spoke for all of us. The Tunnel attendant, still with his head in the car, looked around, frowning.

'Quel est c'est odeur?'

I looked in ignorance at Anna.

Anna sniffed. I sniffed. As dog owners, we have quite a high tolerance level when it comes to smell, but there was a stink of something pungent. It was certainly strong enough to have alerted staff and directed them to our vehicle. This was more serious than one of Matilda's blow-offs.

'Oh Monsieur,' Anna suddenly relaxed and broke into a smile.

'C'est tripe, Monsieur! Le green tripe!'

We will never know if it was assumed the offal was for our own consumption, the French having such sophisticated palates and so little regard for British taste, but the urgency of getting the rapidly thawing dog food into a fridge gave us an extra incentive to arrive in Paris as quickly as possible.

Anna's expertise on autoroutes was impressive, even in the dark. I took control of navigation and had the map spread on my lap, and the use of a Tourist Torch for Tricky Doggy Trips, which was attached to Molly's lead.

'Keep right, no sorry, second exit, oh blast, I meant first.' I shouted conflicting directions to Anna. Unfortunately, I had set us on the road to the Belgian border. Anna kept her cool and, thankfully, it's a universal truth that dogs are not back-seat drivers. While I was embarrassed at my incompetence, they continued to enjoy looking at the passing lorries and flashing lights. A quick turn around at a service station put us back on track.

Nothing was going to wind us up. As a dog lover, there is something so much more enjoyable about travelling if your dog is with you. Even after we had taken the wrong route, we just laughed and stopped to let the dogs pee before continuing on our way. Matilda, who generally snores throughout car trips, was sitting alongside Molly, concentrating on the route ahead.

As we entered Paris, Anna got more and more French. It was a complete transformation. She tied her hair up in a bun and stuck a pencil in it while still driving. She swore in French at the traffic, ignored one-way systems and asked if I'd packed a beret! She had one hand on the horn and the other on the wheel, and we sped through the city comme la Thelma et la Louise.

Instinct or memory guided her to our destination. We arrived in the Marais district at 3 a.m., all four of us tired but enthusiastic, and screeched to a halt right outside the hotel. A few minutes later, laden down with bags and dogs, we staggered into the dimly lit reception area. Three elderly locals looked up from playing poker. They were puffing on Gauloise, under the NO SMOKING sign. One of them, on seeing us, let his fag droop from his mouth and said, 'Aagh, les chiens ...'

'Qui evidement,' snapped Anna, eager to let them know she understood every word.

In his own time, the old boy stood up and led us to our rooms. It was a typical three-star Parisian hotel, clean and, like most others in the city, dog friendly. We had booked two double rooms with French shutters and balconies overlooking the Rue de Bretagne.

Exhausted from the day and the hot May air, Matilda and I flopped the moment we entered our room. She in frog pose with her nose on the balcony, and me onto a soft double bed. I looked up at the ceiling, enjoying the breeze through the open shutters, the room lit only by the lamps from the silent street below.

Comfortable hotels are always sexy to me. There is nothing as wasteful as a single occupant in a hotel double room. Tonight, however, listening to Matilda's snores and chilling from our trip across the channel, a bed all to myself was just what I wanted. I pummelled the continental bolster firmly behind my head and anticipated a few hours of uneventful, gorgeous sleep.

I should have called George but I couldn't move. My phone was in the case on the other side of the room but it could have been miles away. I had not the energy even to sit up. Besides, I thought, nodding off, he would be in a brandy-soaked slumber, adrift on our Marylebone platform bed, snoring into his pillow. I would call him in the morning after a delicious, leisurely breakfast of confiture, croissant, café au lait ... my eyelids closed as counting sheep was replaced with French vocabulary. Assiette ... serviette ... la tasse ... it did the trick. Sleep beautiful sleep.

'Merdre! L'imbecile!' I was awoken by an almighty screech and shouting from the street below.

'Where the hell am I?' I thought, sitting up. The bolster helped me remember, and sun was streaming in, but the hum of Parisian traffic was being blasted out by what must have been a single hand pressed continually on a car horn. The voices were becoming more and more irate. Then another, sharper horn was competing with the first.

'Oh no,' I thought, as it reached a crescendo. 'If this is going to happen every morning, I'm going to insist on changing rooms.'

Pushing Matilda off the bed, I stomped grumpily to look over the balcony and immediately saw the problem. Our mini was parked illegally, and at an angle, preventing any traffic from passing down the narrow street. Standing in front of it, writing a ticket, was a gendarme. Holding up the car's rear end and trying to manoeuvre it were two irate shopkeepers. They all looked cross. We must have been more exhausted last night than we had realized.

I ran into the corridor, accompanied by an excited Matilda, and banged on Anna's door.

'Wake up! Anna, wake up! Gendarme! Gendarme! We have to move the car!' The sound of grunts came from within. 'Meet me downstairs with the car keys. Hurry,' I shouted. 'I'll try and calm them all down.'

I shoved Matilda back into my room, pulled on a sweater over my sweat pants and ran into the street. Somehow I knew this was going to be more tricky than attempting to bribe a Westminster traffic warden.

'Pardon! Pardon, Messieurs, pardon!' I'd used up all my French vocabulary as I confronted the gendarme. He stuck his ticket in my hand and started to walk away, leaving the two sweaty men holding my car up by the bumper. Gestures truly do speak volumes and theirs pretty much summed up their mood.

'Please don't try to move my car,' I pleaded. 'My friend, she is on the way. Messieurs, mon amie, she will move the car.'

At that moment the hotel front door swung open.

'Oh shit!' We all turned in that direction, even the disappearing gendarme, and stared at what I can only describe as a type of canine tableau.

Anna, still half asleep, in sunglasses, blonde hair sticking up in a bouffant with the pencil, was wearing a massive nightshirt with Molly's face on it. And clogs. Molly, as usual, was by her side, also wearing a nightshirt, with her own face on it, but her shirt was dripping wet. Molly appeared also to be wearing one boot. We all stopped shouting to take in this vision of the dishevelled blonde with her bull terrier in a wet T-shirt.

The angry group parted, the gendarme continued on his way and Anna, Molly and I got in the car and set off in search of a car park.

'The air conditioning in my room isn't working,' she said. 'Molly and I were suffocating. I had to put her in a wet T-shirt to cool her down, and her corn needed dressing.'

'Why didn't you open the French windows?' I asked. 'Matilda and I slept with a wonderful breeze.'

'No, I never have windows or doors open, in case Molly decides to go on the run,' Anna said. 'She's a terrier and she can be very terrier-like.'

Aside from the roof in Marylebone, this was my first introduction to Anna's neurosis about Molly running off. It's a subject that recurs frequently throughout our friendship. In fact, once we had started filming the reality series, one episode that highlighted this neurosis actually determined our success. At the time, though, I had to bite my tongue and not criticize what I thought was over-protectiveness.

I was learning that Anna would take any amount of attitude from people, but if someone, like the surly poker player when we arrived, or a situation, like an open window, threatened Molly, she would react. There is no reasoning. I sometimes see others question it, as probably Y Bother had, but I never do. Molly tests Anna's fears quite frequently. It's what makes the two of them so fascinating. Both of them know it's attention seeking.

That first morning, after the car-parking episode, we wandered in to the café next door for breakfast, a family-run business. Tables were spread along the pavement and a bevy of young waiters hovered attentively. One of them fell to his knees when he spotted Molly and Matilda.

'You have beautiful dogs,' he said. 'Let me squeeze the faces. I fetch them some water and maybe some sausage, Mesdames.' We grabbed an outside table in the sun. This was the life.

'Now I'm among my own people ...' said Anna, producing a packet of Gauloise and lighting up. I'd never seen her smoke in public before, maybe it was a French thing. When our waiter returned, he found two other waiters kneeling on the ground, fussing over us as well as the dogs. Three attractive young men appeared to be grovelling at our feet.

At the next table, an elderly lady, wearing a panama hat and white gloves, was feeding dried sausage to a chihuahua. The dog was seated in her handbag, which she had placed on the table. Watching all the attention our dogs were attracting, she leaned over and whispered, 'You should let them off their ropes, Mesdames, let them be free. They will be happier being free.' She waved her hands at us to untie the dogs.

Anna would have lain face down in the road before ever letting Molly off the lead, but I felt it rude to decline the invitation, so I unclipped Matilda. She wandered straight into the kitchen, and soon we heard nothing but cries of delight.

'We must drink a glass of Cinquante et Un,' suggested Anna, lighting another cigarette. 'I got quite a taste for it when I lived here. It's pastis with a touch of grenadine. Delicious.'

Sitting outside the café, we had ringside seats for the Saturday flea market, which was being set out all along the street. Hundreds of stalls, on either side of the road, selling vintage jewellery, clothes, shoes and paintings.

One stall, close to our table, was in the care of a quite weathered and attractive grey-haired man, wearing a cheesecloth shirt and shorts. He had hung a beautiful Chinese rug over a fire hydrant to mark his pitch, draped another along a bench and was lying on top of it, sunbathing. Most of the stallholders were tanned, hippy types, laughing, smoking and chatting to each other with no sense of profiteering.

An afternoon of blissful bargain-hunting stretched ahead. We sat in the sunshine, soaking it all in.

'Cheers,' I said. 'Let's raise a toast to the screen test next week.' The drink Anna had ordered was strong and tasted of aniseed. It reminded me of Pernod. Lovely, but one would be enough.

'I hope we're going to look all right on camera,' Anna said. 'I'm not worried about Molly. She loves a lens.'

Matilda and I would both benefit from a bit of botox.

'We would have to be pretty dire for them not to want us,' I said, lifting my face up to the sun. 'They seemed so keen to pin us down with dates. I emailed them another couple of videos.'

'I'm hoping Molly's corn will have gone by then,' said Anna. 'I've also booked to get my roots done.'

I suddenly remembered that I hadn't texted George. I hadn't even turned my phone on since leaving the UK. I sat bolt upright, fished about in my handbag and pulled out my phone. There was one text. It was from George. He'd sent it the night before: MISS MY TWO GIRLS. HATE BEING HERE WITHOUT YOU.

I went to retrieve Matilda from the adoring staff in the kitchen and ordered two more Cinquante et Uns on the way. The taste was growing on me.

I knew all along that George would be lost without us and wondered how he would be spending his day. Maybe he'd be sitting in Bar Italia or photographing buildings. Most weekends it was usually me who made all the plans and he willingly fitted in with them. Theatre, films, dinners – he enjoyed anything as long as I was there, but they were always my choices. I was beginning to feel guilty, because I really had no idea what he would do when left to his own devices. Maybe the brandy I'd hidden under the duvet would give him a lift. I decided to call him later that evening, from my room, before dinner.

Back at our table I found Anna chatting away in fluent French to the lady with the chihuahua. Her dog was still in her bag on the table, but fast asleep with its head in the bread basket. Matilda lay in the shade under my chair. Molly was sitting on Anna's lap à la the number 19 bus position. The two women gesticulated, exaggerated and enthused with no apparent language barrier, and I listened, enviously, for any part of the conversation that I might be able to translate.

'Serge Gainsbourg et Jane Birkin habitait à tout près d'ici. Leurs chiens etait presque la même que votre bull terrier et la bulldog de votre amie,' said chihuahua lady.

Anna hugged Molly with sheer joy and swung round to face me.

'No wonder we're getting so much attention,' she explained. 'This lovely lady has just told me that Serge Gainsbourg and Jane Birkin lived round the corner from here and they had exactly the same combination of bull breeds as we do. A brown bull terrier and a white bulldog. They were often seen walking them through the Marais. I loved Serge Gainsbourg!'

So did I. He died in 1991 but I'd recently seen a film starring their daughter, Charlotte. What a beautiful family!

'Ask her if Jane Birkin still lives near here,' I said.

Apparently, she did, in the same house, and still had a bulldog. Paris was becoming more and more fabulous by the hour. We both agreed we must walk past Jane Birkin's house with Molly and Matilda, just in case. It was a slim chance she would invite us in, but a glimpse of her dog would do.

Anna was also insistent we visit Rin Tin Tin's grave that afternoon. It was just outside the city. We had so much we wanted to do but only the two days to fit everything in. We ordered two more Cinquant et Uns.

The market was now busy and shoppers were having to squeeze past our table. Every so often a local would ask politely for permission to photograph the dogs. A couple of blokes even requested that we pose alongside them. Where would these pictures be shown?

The city was full of stunning-looking, stylish people, but the four of us were being bathed in glances of appreciation and we weren't used to it. Women of every generation, especially with dogs, really do have a value in Paris. For Anna and I, sitting in the Rue de Bretagne, in the glorious sunshine, slightly squiffy, receiving so much attention made us feel as vital as a pair of young Bardots.

I'd noticed the tanned, Chinese-rug man had been paying our table a lot of attention, and he seemed particularly taken with Anna. He hadn't sold a thing but spent his time chatting to the elderly chihuahua lady, and he held her elbow as she tottered past his stall on her way home. He climbed back on his makeshift rug bed and returned his gaze to Molly. We settled our bill and as we made our way between the stalls, he smiled at Molly, put his hand under her chin and then patted her.

'She is a beautiful dog,' he said in almost perfect English, looking at Anna. 'I hear you want to visit the house of Serge Gainsbourg. You are in luck. I was his friend. I looked after his bull terrier when he was away filming.'

His eyes were deep turquoise blue and he was wearing a matching bead necklace. Very St Tropez.

'I bet he has an awful lot of Shirley Valentines under his belt,' I thought.

For Anna, however, his opening gambit of a speech was pure aphrodisiac. Anyone who praised Molly was in with a chance. She lent towards him and whispered, 'Don't suppose you know where the grave is of Rin Tin Tin?'

That stumped him. It was as though she'd asked him directions to a strip club.

'Who is Mr Rin Tin Tin?' he asked.

'A beautiful creature who became a film star,' enthused Anna. 'He's buried in Paris. I would love to sit by his grave.'

'I am sorry to hear about Mr Rin Tin Tin,' said the rug man. 'Mais Madame, I would be honoured to show you and your friend the house of Jane Birkin this evening.'

'We are off to explore the sights, Monsieur,' replied Anna. 'But thank you, and may I say how beautiful your rugs are.'

We gathered the dogs around us and set off through the market.

'You've just been hit upon,' I grinned. 'Blimey. Bit different to the blokes in Brick Lane.'

'Any friend of Serge's is a friend of mine,' she giggled. 'Don't know about you but I'm feeling a bit drunk.'

My phone made me jump – a picture text had arrived. I knew it would be from George. He would send me photos throughout the day. Not all of them informative. I clicked onto it and up flashed a picture of a plate of fried food. Underneath he had written 'my breakfast'. I studied it to see if I recognized the plate. It wouldn't be one of mine because I didn't have any but I should be able to identify the crockery of his local haunts. Unfortunately, I couldn't.

We spent the rest of the afternoon walking, then stopping at a café for more pastis, a bowl of water for the dogs, a photograph for the admirers and a cigarette for Anna before setting back on our way. As we neared the main shopping area with department stores and perfumeries, I became very animated and suggested we do some clothes shopping and maybe get some cologne for George. If I got his present now, I thought I'd feel less guilty.

'We can do all that after we've been to the cemetery,' agreed Anna. 'But first we should get to the north of the city and lay flowers on the grave of one of the bravest of wartime dogs, Rin Tin Tin. After that, we'll feel energized.'

Now, given the option of shopping for clothes in the Champs Elysées or sitting over a dog's grave, there was no contest. Anna and I shared a lot in common but her obsession with this dead dog puzzled me. Alcohol had made her bold and instead of me and my bossiness taking charge, it was she who was determined to lead the four of us on a pilgrimage.

The Cimetière des Chiens (cemetery for dogs) is on the north-west side of Paris, a metro ride away. The nearest stop is Gabriel Péri. The sun and the Cinquant et Uns had stupefied us and we were hardly capable of a lengthy walk, let alone handling a trip on the metro.

'Taxi,' we cried in unison.

'Well that's the budget blown on one simple journey,' I thought as we bundled the dogs in.

The taxi driver pulled up at the main gate.

'But it's for dead animals,' he grunted. 'Bonne chance!' Then he drove off.

The words Cimetière des Chiens and the date 1899 were carved into a massive arch supported by two stone pillars. The place reminded me of London's Nunhead or Highgate Cemeteries. Gothic decay. We paid our 3½ euros, were given a brochure and a map and went in through the side gate.

Nothing in the information handed to us was new to Anna. She probably could have written it herself such was her knowledge of the place. She seemed to know instinctively where to explore, and she set off through the graves, Molly trotting by her side.

Matilda and I strolled around, absorbing the history of the extraordinary surroundings while I consulted the brochure. Here was an example of the French love for animals. Founded in 1888, the cemetery was created to comply with laws insisting that animals be buried at least 100 meters away from dwellings. Soon it became a respected resting place for pets, although its future was in jeopardy until 1987, when it was granted permanent status. Now, as well as graves, it has monuments to pet dogs, brave army dogs, cats, police horses and even a monkey called Kiki.

The cemetery consists of two large gardens on different levels, filled with oak trees, palms and tumbling jasmine. The tranquillity and peace instantly drew me in. Human graveyards are thought-provoking places but the Cimetière des Chiens is different. It's sadder. Inscriptions such as 'N'oublerais jamais' (I will never forget you) and 'Mon ami fidele' (my loyal companion) are hidden beneath flowering shrubs. One grave had a plastic globe containing tennis balls and the inscription 'Henri, who loved to chase a ball'. A mausoleum made of stone, featuring a First World War dog carrying a boy on his back, had written on it 'The 41st. He carried 40 to safety and died after the 41st'. Next to it, a pink plaster poodle draped in plastic pearls adorned a grave bearing the message 'Bibi, who lives on in Mardi Gras' – beautiful, camp sentiment among the graves of animal war heroes. A bull terrier from New York City, Oscar, lies buried here, surrounded by 'yellow cab' licence plates.

Matilda walked respectfully by my side. Did she know we were walking among the resting place of her own species? The sun had gone in and the lights of the city were shining through the trees. If I was feeling teary, I could only guess what kind of emotional state Anna would be in. I now understood her insistence on making the pilgrimage.

I walked towards a kitsch, ornamental fountain and there she was, blonde head bent over a grave, Molly sitting as sentry by her side.

'Look,' she said. And there it was. 'The grave of Rin Tin Tin'.

A colour photograph of a handsome German shepherd dog drew the eye. It was glued to a stick that had been pushed into the ground above the well-tended grave. Fresh yellow flowers bloomed in vases on all four sides, amid other floral tributes, presumably left by loving fans.

I had always assumed Rin Tin Tin was a manifestation of Hollywood. Until I met Anna, I had no idea he was real.

'He was a brave and clever trench dog from the First World War,' she told me, patting Molly. 'He rescued many soldiers, and then he was adopted by an American soldier who took him to Hollywood, where he ended up earning more than Garbo.'

I'm not sure if it was the exhaustion, the alcohol or the emotion of the moment but when Anna looked up at me, tears were running down her face.

'I want Molly to be buried here,' she said.

My phone started to ring. It might be George and I needed to speak to him.

'Anna,' I replied, 'let's not think about that now. We're here in Paris. We're having fun. A sexy rug seller wants to take you out. Let's not talk about anyone dying.'

The phone would soon go to voicemail if I didn't answer it.

'You have to understand,' she said. 'I need to know where Molly will be buried. It's so important. I live in a London flat with no real garden. Here in Paris is where I was happiest. One day I may live here again and, if I do, I can visit Molly in this cemetery. She will be buried alongside one of the bravest dogs in history. It's what she deserves.'

I looked at Matilda, lying sprawled like a frog on the path. She was still young. It had never occurred to me to plan her burial. Molly looked at Anna, who was now lying across the grave, sobbing. Her dog really did seem to clock her moods.

'Anna, I think you've had too much to drink. Please. It's all going to be all right.' I did my best to pacify her. Then I answered the phone.

'Hello,' I whispered.

'Watcha! How are my girls?' bellowed George. He sounded odd. 'Did you get the pic of my breakfast?'

'Where are you?'

'Where are you?'

'In a graveyard,' I said. 'For dogs. It's getting a bit emotional actually. How are things?'

'You're in a graveyard? Jeez … thought you'd be in a bar by now. I'm in the flat watchin' telly.'

I moved away a little from Anna and Molly.

'It's a bit tricky here to be honest,' I whispered. 'Anna's taken a turn over the grave of Rin Tin Tin.'

I heard George's snigger.

'Told you she was barking. Call me when you get back to the hotel, before you go to sleep.' And he rung off.

I looked down at my friend, who was now embracing the grave's entire floral display with her body.

'Come on, Anna. Molly has years left in her. Besides, the number of supplements you shove down her throat, she'll outlive all of us.'

Anna hauled herself up, dirt all over her tie-dye top, sat on her heels and stared at her dog.

'I love her beyond anyone else,' she said. 'She is the longest relationship I have ever had. Boyfriends are a pain, but for a decade, Molls has relied on me and me on her. She is, in our language, "Sensals".'

I looked puzzled.

'It means sensational,' she continued. 'Molly knows everything about me. She's my pilot through life. I don't need anyone or anything else.'

There, she had admitted it. Molly turned her gaze to me as if to say, 'Told you.'

We sat there, silently, gazing at the cut-out photo of a famous German shepherd dog, mounted on a stick in a graveyard. The city traffic hummed below. My head was beginning to ache.

Another text arrived on my phone. I clicked onto it. A picture of a full bottle of brandy and the words 'My dinner'.

It was almost dark as I helped Anna back to her feet.

'Well, we've missed the shops,' I said. 'We'll have to go shopping tomorrow.'

'Impossible,' said Anna. 'We're booked in to be wormed.'

That evening, back at the hotel, I tried calling George. It went to voicemail. I hung up. What was he up to? Earlier, he had sounded distracted and over casual. He and I never made cursory calls. We either enthused or rowed over the phone but we were never polite. Even miles away from home, his big bombastic presence was pummelling away in my mind. I knocked on Anna's door to see if she had heard from Y Bother.

Her room was identical to mine but the atmosphere couldn't have been more different. There was almost no sign of Anna occupying the room; instead, it had become a homage to Molly. The carpet was littered with more hooves than a farmyard, some chewed, others still fresh. Three types of feeding bowls were by the dressing table, which itself was covered in Molly's supplements. Molly's travelling bed along with what looked like her own linen was next to Anna's. I couldn't believe they had spent just one night here. It looked as though they had lived in this room for years.

'Have you heard from Y Bother?' I asked.

Anna was filing Molly's corn – a weekly procedure. Corns were caused by a design fault in bull terriers' feet, so I'd been told. Once filed, Molly's foot would be covered in an unction and left to soak overnight in a boot.

'Who?' asked Anna. 'Oh no, I don't think so. I haven't turned my phone on.' Then she added, 'I hope he remembers to water my plants. If the weather is the same back home as it is here, they'll dry out.'

She laced up Molly's boot and reached for her phone. There was one voicemail.

'It's a photographer,' she said as she listened. 'He's a contact of mine and has agreed to photograph us at the vet's tomorrow. English bloke but lives here in Paris.'

'Why?' I asked. 'Why are we being photographed by a professional at the vet's?'

'I agreed to get some pics for *Dogs Daily* magazine. They're running a feature on pet passports. Exploring the pros and cons,' she replied. 'They just need shots of the girls in the surgery. We can get pics of the tablets, their mouths and the passports. Oh and, hopefully, the vet. Should look good.'

Such was the ingenuity of Anna. Placements in magazines were good for the pet products she dealt with. If she could include them in photos she was supplying for a feature article, so much the better. Everyone benefited.

She had already filled me in with a few details. Back then, in order to be allowed back into the UK, pets had to be wormed no more than 48 hours, but at least 24 hours, before departure. Rules were relaxed a few years later, so now the tick and flea treatment is no longer required.

It left us a very tight window of opportunity and meant that most of our second and final day in France would be spent at the only vet's to be found open on a Sunday.

'When we get there, you have to follow my instructions,' said Anna. 'I'm worried the spot-on tick treatment they administer might be bad for the dogs. What if it gets into their bloodstream? We should take a bottle of water with us and as we leave the surgery throw the water over the dogs' necks to wash it off.'

'Isn't that illegal?' I asked.

'Not if the treatment's been professionally applied and the passport stamped. But we'll have to act quickly, before the stuff sinks in.'

I never really know if Anna's fanaticism over Molly's welfare is neurosis or informed. But I don't question it. Since I met her, Matilda's vet's fees have decreased, she eats only raw food and I believe she's more energetic. So this eccentric course of action at the vet's seemed to be a good plan.

Anna had arranged to meet the photographer, Phil, in the waiting room. Before he arrived, our only companion was a man with a balding parrot. The bird kept pulling its feathers out and chucking them all over the floor. Molly was giving it the evil eye; Matilda's radar had closed down and she was asleep on the floor. The sight of the stressed bird was unsettling Anna.

'Monsieur,' she began, leaning towards the parrot owner.

'No,' I butted in. 'Please don't start extoling the virtues of royal jelly. I can tell just by looking at this bloke it won't wash.'

Anna lent back in her chair, knocked into submission. Phil the photographer came stumbling in through the waiting-room door. He must have had three cameras slung over his neck. Either he'd come from a very important shoot or this vet picture was a bigger deal than I thought.

'Ma petite Anna,' he said. 'How are you, girl? Good to see you. Which one of these is yours? Where are you staying?'

Anna giggled and appeared to flirt, so I assumed Phil was one of her past conquests. He had the look of the rogue about him.

The lady vet appeared and ushered the parrot and its owner through to the surgery. She was extremely glamorous, wearing a pencil skirt and what looked like false eyelashes.

'Blimey,' I said to Anna and Phil. 'She can't be expecting to stick her arm up many cow's bottoms.'

'Tell me what you want when we get in there,' said Phil. 'I was thinking of action shots.'

'Do you live here in Paris?' I asked him.

'I've been here for thirty years,' he replied. 'I'm a news photographer – used to work for Reuters. Covered all the big stories. The biggest, of course, was the death of Diana. I could tell you loads of unpublished details about that night,' he added.

'And now you're covering worming stories,' I thought. 'Must be a slow news day.'

The parrot man came out of the surgery, sans parrot.

'Bonjour, entrez vous,' said glamorous vet.

'Merci Madame. Le photographer, qui s'appelait Phil, va prendre les photos quand vous ferez les traitements contre les vers.'

Anna explained that Phil would be taking photographs during the procedure. I'm sure this didn't phase the vet. She was more than camera ready. 'Done up like a dog's dinner' my mother would have called her. I don't think any professional in Paris did 'casual'.

I let Anna take charge. For all my bossiness, I knew when to hand over the reins.

There seemed to be very little photographic mileage in giving two dogs two worming tablets and then applying tick lotion round the neck. But Phil seemed very committed and Anna was directing all of us with as much efficiency as if it was a TV commercial.

'Madame, please hold your hand like this on Molly's neck,' she said. 'Now Madame, please can we have a close-up of you stamping the passport?'

If the vet was finding our behaviour bizarre, then our departure must have seemed even more absurd. We had insisted on paying for the treatment prior to the appointment, ensuring a rapid getaway. As soon as the vet had meticulously applied the spot-on formula to Molly's neck, Anna leapt towards the open surgery door.

'Merci, Madame, merci. Vite, Molly, vite!' She shoved Molly out of the door.

I watched as the spot-on was applied to Matilda's neck. The door burst open and Anna's head and shoulders appeared round it.

'Vite, Jo, vite!' she shouted.

We charged out of the veterinary practice as though we had raided it. Outside the front door Anna produced a bottle of water from up her sleeve and chucked it all over our surprised dogs as well as Phil's feet.

'What the hell ...?' he exclaimed, emptying his sandals.

'It had to be done,' said Anna, showing no inclination to apologize. 'I did it for the health of our dogs. We don't want a picture of it, Phil.'

'Excuse me, you forgot these.'

The vet had followed us through the front door and was holding the pet passports. She had missed the action. All she saw were two drenched dogs and a photographer removing his sandals. With her hands on her svelte hips she attempted to interpret the situation. Quick-thinking Phil, balancing on one leg joked, 'Oh Madame, les Anglaises! They are jokers, eh!'

I moved towards her, smiling. 'Merci, Madame,' I said, taking the passports. 'A bientôt.'

Our return journey back to the UK was far less relaxed. We had barely managed to cover all that was on Anna's wish list. The worming of the dogs had taken up more time than we had allowed.

Before departure, we returned to the cemetery because Anna wanted to book a plot for Molly. Given the choice of a French grave for Matilda or one in London, I didn't really want to think about it.

We held our breath going through pet passport control at Calais. The family ahead of us had mistimed their worming session and had to get their retriever urgently to a vet near the port.

Molly and Matilda passed through without a problem and 40 minutes later we were back in Folkestone. As we emerged from the tunnel, both of our phones started firing out alert sounds informing us of texts, voicemails and missed calls.

'Merdre,' sighed Anna. 'We're back.'

'None of these are from George,' I said, going through my messages. 'Not a picture of a meal, a text or voicemail. Strange. Maybe when I get home, he'll be fast asleep in bed. Anything from Y Bother?'

'No,' she answered. 'These are all work related. I'll go through them later.'

Anna had put her phone on speaker while she was driving and it clicked on to an incoming voicemail.

'Hi, this is Hannah. From Pulse Films. We're looking forward to filming you girls and Molly and Matilda tomorrow for the screen test. We were thinking of having the four of you taking afternoon tea, with the dogs joining in. Is there anywhere you hang out? Could you suggest anywhere?'

'The Milestone!' we shouted out in unison.

The Milestone Hotel in Knightsbridge was dog friendly. Anna and I would go there with the dogs for special occasions, or just to cheer ourselves up. Our spirits started to rise.

We dropped Anna and Molly off outside her Islington flat. I was too concerned about getting back home to notice if her window boxes had been watered. As Matilda and I opened the front door to my flat I held my breath. Would George still be asleep? Would the tiny place be in mayhem?

Matilda rushed passed me, tail wagging in anticipation of seeing George sitting there. It was her sudden standing to attention that alerted me that things weren't quite right. She looked as confused as I felt. Nothing had been moved. Everything was as I'd left it. No dropped clothes, abandoned guitars or washing-up. I moved towards the bed and put my hand under the duvet. The half bottle of brandy I'd hidden was still there. He hadn't slept in the bed.

I dialled Anna's number and it seemed to ring for ages.

'Hello,' she said.

'It's me,' I said. 'Something odd's happened.'

'You're not kidding,' she replied. 'Y Bother has left me. All he's left is a note.'

CHAPTER 3

'We need a close-up on the gusset.'

'WE ARE ALL PROSTITUTES' is written on my oldest T-shirt, and I wore it with irony throughout the 80s. Thirty years later, filming *A Different Breed*, the words seemed more appropriate.

From the moment we'd been told Pulse Films were considering us for their new series, Anna and I had become terrier-like in our determination to appear in it. The success of the radio show had made us bold as well as ambitious, and we would have sold our souls to the devil for a bit of telly action.

A young, excited researcher had phoned to explain the format. Over the course of eight episodes, the bizarre world of dog ownership, through the eyes of the dogs rather than their owners, would be played out. Strong characters with intriguing storylines were essential. Some of the dogs would have self-op cameras attached to their collars and be dubbed with human voices. The origin of the breed would be reflected in the accents. Italian greyhounds would speak with an Italian accent, for example, and Westies would have a Scottish lilt. Nothing in television, we were told, had ever been made like it before. Each week, new characters would be introduced into the central storylines, but a small core were to be used in every episode. It was hinted that Anna and I might be two of them. George's many videos, along with the radio show, had, definitely, paved the way. Everything now rested on the screen test.

The Milestone is a five-star Knightsbridge hotel that welcomes dogs. It's one of the city's few remaining private hotels and the owner's yellow labrador lives with him on the top floor. In the early days of our radio show, we'd interviewed the manager and recorded a tour of the facilities for an item on 'Travelling in Luxury with your Pets in London'. They like us and we knew they would repay the favour by permitting filming.

Taking tea at the Milestone seemed the perfect backdrop for the screen test and the classy surroundings would, hopefully, reflect on us. We were certain the crew would be impressed.

The main entrance overlooks Hyde Park and liveried doormen wait to welcome guests at the top of the grand steps. They accompany dogs throughout the building and are on call to walk and exercise them at the owner's request. A dog-sitting service operates for all rooms.

Unlike Paris, where our dogs had access to all areas, even the kitchens, here dogs are restricted to certain public lounges.

The Pavilion Tearoom is one of them. Leading off the main hall and designed in the black-and-white style of Cecil Beaton, it has an ornate marble floor and mirror and glass walls, two of which are covered floor to ceiling with black-and-white stills of Marilyn Monroe. Tropical ferns and cacti cascade from hanging baskets. The place looks for all the world like a glamorous film set, and although we were later told it's a nightmare to film in, the results are gorgeous to look at.

The perfect cream teas, served in bone china and on five-layer cake stands, are as theatrical as the surroundings. A designated doggy menu offers dishes such as the woof waffle – a Cumberland sausage in a waffle bathed in a red wine jus – all served in a silver bowl.

Anna and I decided to meet 15 minutes before the arrival of the crew so we could settle the dogs as well as our minds. We'd done ourselves up like a pair of dogs' dinners and had on silk tea dresses, stilettos and red lipstick. Matilda and Molly were in matching collars.

The excited researcher had kept the brief ... well ... brief. 'Our executive producer along with a cameraman would like to film the four of you having tea, yeah? Just do what you usually do at the gaffe, right? Won't take longer than an hour, yeah? Just be cool and when they start filming, act normal, right?'

'What's normal?' asked Anna, looking slightly frayed. 'Molly will devour the waffle in one bite. If the camera isn't on her at that moment, there'll be nothing left to film.'

'I suppose they want to watch our interaction with the dogs as well as each other,' I said.

Our trip to Paris had done nothing to relax us. Returning to London to discover there was trouble with the menfolk was a bit of a shock. Y Bother had fled Islington, leaving only a note. I had yet to learn what he had written, but as it was on the back of an invoice from Mobile Petfoods, it can't have been lengthy.

Big George had spent two nights away from our flat but was pretending he hadn't. I could easily have asked where he had been but something prevented me. Either I was protecting him, or I was protecting myself from knowing. Instead, I removed the half bottle of brandy I'd hidden in the bed and behaved as though nothing was wrong. It meant there was a slight sense of strain between us.

Sitting waiting for the crew to arrive, Anna and I were getting more and more wound up. The hotel staff, all dressed in morning suits, had been told to wait until everyone had arrived before taking orders and fussing around us. Anna, as always in a stressful situation, was having a conversation in her own language with Molly.

'We doin our doins Nood, and we goin do our bestals in the hotelels and the waffles and the doins Nuood.'

It's surprising how much of their language I'm able to identify. There must be a code that subliminally enters the brain. I've almost cracked it.

I never doubted Anna's entertainment value, or Molly's, who had won endless rosettes for her talent. But looking at Matilda, already asleep and snoring, showing not an ounce of adrenalin, and myself, a control freak, I began to question my role in the project.

I'd spent 12 years as a presenter with my own radio show. Unlike Anna, who behaved purely from instinct, I'd become guarded about how I was perceived. Behind the microphone I felt safe and protected from unpredictable situations because I controlled what came out of the speakers. Guests on our show talked for as long as I allowed them to; if they led us into uncomfortable areas or, as occasionally happened, dried up, I could end the interview. The short documentaries I filmed were directed and scripted. If we were to land this gig, the thought of having my every move, expression and comment filmed, panicked me. I would have to learn to adapt. Matilda, unlike Molly, had no party tricks. She was either awake or snoring. Most days found her looking like a bored Margaret Rutherford to Molly's snooty Edith Sitwell.

'I'm going to phone Julian,' I decided.

Anna smiled. 'What, for some advice on how we should conduct ourselves? Good idea.'

'No,' I replied. 'To ask if he would join us here for tea.'

A theatrical expression I once heard describes beautifully the director's solution to a tricky situation in a film. If he has tried, and exhausted, every ploy but can't find the perfect ending to a scene, he will say, 'Let's throw the lot at the wall.' In other words, 'Gather every bit of ammunition we have, throw it out there and see what happens.'

Well, Julian Clary would be our ammunition. As long as he was willing, and in London, we would throw him into the mix. I dialled his number. He answered.

'Hello,' I said. 'I don't suppose you would consider joining Anna and I for a slap-up tea in Knightsbridge? You can bring the dogs.'

'Oh how lovely,' he said in his gentle voice. 'I'm stuck in Camden writing at the moment. When would you like me?'

'Now?' I answered quickly. 'Oh, and Julian, would you mind if a film crew filmed it?'

Silence.

'It's a screen test for the reality series I told you about, Julian. We don't think we are interesting enough.'

Silence.

'It's just that if we got it, Molly and Matilda will be on film for perpetuity. They will be forever on celluloid. It's for them really, more than for us.'

'Order me a cucumber sandwich,' he said and asked for the address.

The crew's arrival was something of a surprise. They looked like children to us. The executive producer, Hannah, was probably in her early 30s, very punk chic, wearing a faux fur stole.

The cameraman was in his early 20s and the female researcher, Sophie, looked 12. They couldn't have been more different from my BBC documentary team.

I noticed that Sophie was hesitant about coming into the room. She was hanging about near the door, holding a clipboard.

'I'm a bit scared of dogs,' she said, pulling the sleeves of her cardigan over her hands. Anna and I looked at each other.

'Our dogs are very friendly,' reassured Anna, bringing Molly forward. 'Say hello, Molly.'

Molly, right on cue, threw back her head and barked. Sophie retreated round the door.

The rest of the crew were very enthusiastic about the location. There was a little concern about the camera being caught in reflection in all the mirrors, but as this was a pilot, not to be used for transmission, it seemed they could work round it.

'How often do you come here?' asked Hannah.

'Oh not that ...' began Anna.

'Most weeks,' I jumped in, 'depending on our diaries.'

There, I'd done it! I'd stretched the truth. Actually, I'd lied. A voice in my head said they will love you both more if they think you can afford to come here every week. Anna, the most honest person in the world, turned to look at me and I avoided her eye.

'So,' said Hannah. 'We're ready. Don't even think about us, just carry on in the way you usually do. Ignore us. We're not here. She sat herself on a chaise-longue-styled sofa and Sophie, mustering up courage, still holding her clipboard, crept in beside her.

Anna and I sat parallel, a few feet away, on our sofa, with the two dogs stationed politely by our sides. Trying not to catch the eyes of those sitting opposite, or indeed to look into the camera, left us very little option about where to focus. We both stared, unnaturally, at each other. Everybody was waiting for some kind of action. A lingering waiter we'd never set eyes on before walked into my eyeline. I gestured.

'Oh hello,' I said in an overly familiar fashion. 'Could we have our usual?'

Anna, Molly and Matilda stared at him in anticipation. I smiled, hopefully. He was holding a silver tray and, unlike us, appeared to be completely unperturbed by the camera now focused on him. After a slight pause as he summed up the situation, he replied, 'Certainly, Madame. And the dogs, would they also like their usual?'

'Yes please,' we chorused, with relief.

The camera swung round to follow the exiting waiter, then swung back to rest on the four of us.

'This is pleasant,' said Anna, her hands crossed nicely in her lap.

'Yes,' I echoed, and mimicked her action.

Matilda blew off. The cameraman sniggered.

'Well,' said Anna, after a while, 'shall we see if Molly can offer a paw?'

She sounded a bit like Joyce Grenfell, very posh. Maybe it was the surroundings. Molly ignored Anna and stared right down the camera lens. When the camera moved her eyes followed it.

'Molly, let's show a paw,' said Anna in her new posh voice.

Molly offered a token paw, not looking at Anna, her eyes remaining fixed on the camera.

'Good girl,' said Anna. 'Other paw.'

Half-heartedly, Molly offered the other paw, dropped it back to the ground and continued staring down the lens. The cameraman shifted a little.

'Well, that was good,' I said unnecessarily.

Inside my head I was panicking. I knew enough about TV to realize we were going to have to crank it up a bit to land even one episode let alone eight. All spontaneity had left us. The narrowness of the room and the artificial situation of two women with clipboards sitting on a sofa opposite, seemed to stifle any banter. Molly was obviously scheming, she had that look, and the heat from a combination of glass and lights had sent Matilda to sleep. We were a dull, uninspired little foursome.

In an attempt at creativity, the cameraman turned the camera away and began to film us through the mirror. Molly's eyes followed him. The two girls on the sofa lent back slightly, so as to keep out of shot. I could now see the reflection of the back of our heads and wished I'd opted for a whole head of highlights instead of half.

'Would Molly like to speak?' Anna, eager to rescue the moment, pulled a meatball from her bra. The cameraman wobbled. Molly continued to stare.

'Molly, speak.' Her Joyce Grenfell voice, clipped and anxious, had no effect.

I was now in a panic. Molly's talking was her party trick. It had got us out of so many sticky situations. Refusal to do so would soon have Anna hyperventilating. Visions of a rendition of the dreaded noodle doodle song flooded into my head.

The double doors rattled and we all turned with blessed relief. The waiter was on his way, complete with serving trolley, which he wheeled between the two sofas. Matilda woke up, excited by the sudden yummy smells. Molly finally removed her eyes from the camera and rested them on the trolley. Plates of cucumber and smoked salmon sandwiches were positioned in front of a five-layer cake stand full of mini scones, eclairs, macaroons and sponge fingers.

Behind the trolley walked a footman carrying a tray on which sat two massive silver salvers and a couple of dog bowls. The aroma of meaty casserole filled the salon, heralding the arrival of the woof waffles. Both dogs were now sitting up on full alert. Matilda was drooling on to the carpet. Camera and guests directed their attention to the salvers.

The head waiter placed the two dog bowls next to each other on the floor while the footman held the tray above the dogs' heads. Anna and I were staring, frozen at the theatricality of it all. The camera moved in to take a close-up of the tray and the white gloves of the waiter as he raised the silver lids to reveal the steaming waffles. With full silver service, he placed individual waffles into both bowls on the floor and with a flourish spooned jus over each sausage.

Every mouth in the room was watering. Matilda was virtually in a puddle of saliva, tense with anticipation. Molly turned to Anna for permission to move towards the meal.

'Girls, wait,' said Anna, checking their behaviour. The camera moved to Anna's firm face. 'All right, go.'

They dived towards their bowls and the camera followed. Two mouthfuls and they had each devoured the contents. Please God let the camera have caught it.

What happened next was inevitable if we had just thought it through. Never, ever, feed two dogs side by side, however good friends they are. Molly and Matilda both finished their portions at the same time but, looking enviously at each other's bowls, assumed the other had food left. Matilda attempted to eat from Molly's bowl and Molly, quick as a flash, went for her. Matilda snapped back. Both tried to bite each other's necks! Standing on hind legs the vicious growling and snapping made the cameraman quickly recoil, moving away as far as he could in the restricted space. Sophie let out a small yelp and stood upright on the sofa, the producer did the same and the two of them were now fearfully leaning into each other.

Anna sprang forward, reached into the snarling knot and separated the two of them, putting each one into a 'sit and stay'. The waiter and footman had fled back to the kitchen. I sat like a useless lump in shock and envisioned our potential TV series drifting into the abyss. Both dogs, gravy all over their chins, were panting and grinning. Nobody moved.

'Sorry I'm late.'

We all swung round towards the door to see Julian coming in with his two dogs, Valerie and Albert. The cameraman moved back into the centre of the room and aimed the lens at the newcomers. The girls on the sofa relaxed, stepped back onto the floor and sat down.

'Any tea in the pot?' enquired Julian, elegantly disregarding the camera. 'Have I missed anything?'

He sat in the only remaining armchair with his black matriarchal dog Valerie by his side, and lifted Albert, the younger one, onto his lap. Anna and I, both so relieved to see him, moved forward for a hug.

'Please don't touch me or breathe on me,' he said in his usual fashion, and popped a mini sponge into his mouth.

A few years back, Julian had presented a TV series called *Under Dogs* in which celebrities were taught to train rescue dogs. Anna had worked as a trainer and advisor on the junior version of it. They knew each other well. His dogs always came from rescue and he had only just adopted Albert, via his mate, Paul O'Grady, as a companion for Valerie. Albert was a staffie Jack Russell cross, quite an interesting choice for Julian, who said it made him look as though he should be dealing in heroin rather than humour.

'I wasn't sure whether to arrive through the front or back passage,' he said, reaching for another cake.

More relaxed now by his company, we sat and chatted, drinking tea and learning, from him, to ignore the camera. Whether it was shame or the presence of the newcomers, Molly's and Matilda's behaviour was now exemplary and they lay nicely on the floor.

Lewd innuendos were flying in a constant stream from Julian's mouth, and while Hannah and young Sophie were stifling giggles, I was wondering if the series was a family show. If so, just how much of this adult conversation, even in the pilot episode, could they show? Thinking I could get us back on track by making the topics more family friendly, I launched into the anecdote about how Julian and I had met. Anna had heard this a million times before but I thought it was interesting enough to lead us into a safer conversation.

'We were in panto in Brighton,' I began. 'It was *Cinderella*, I was playing the fairy godmother and Julian was the first-ever male Dandini ...'

Anna started gesturing at me, then waving her hands at the cameraman.

'Don't look,' she hissed pointlessly into the lens. 'Shoo.'

'Each one of his costumes had been individually...' I attempted to continue.

'SHOO!' Anna leant her face straight into the lens. She continued to motion it to move away. Then pointed, then shooed it away again.

'What's the matter?' I asked, incredulous that she could ask a camera to shoo.

She looked at me, then at Julian, and lent in to whisper behind her hand, 'Erection.'

Everyone in the room stared at Julian's lap, including himself. Albert, a mere puppy, oblivious to his physical state, was the culprit. We think it was the sight of the cakes. Julian, quick-thinking as ever, reached forward for an ornamental potted cactus and stuck it in front of the dog's genitals. We could hear the sniggering of the cameraman and the production girls behind us.

'Do excuse him,' said Julian, getting up and putting Albert on the floor. 'He's still quite young.'

Taking it as his cue to go, Julian smiled, politely shook hands with everyone in the room and turned at the door for a final comment, the camera following him.

'This has been the most memorable tea, thank you. I can't remember when I last had so many fingers.'

Then he left.

'CUT!' Hannah the producer stood up. The cameraman put down his camera and wiped his face. Whether he was wiping away sweat or tears, I don't know, but he looked very flushed. Sophie excused herself and scurried out after Julian, claiming she would hail him a taxi but obviously relieved to have an excuse to leave.

Anna and I continued to sit where we were, silent. I could just make out a bite mark appearing over Matilda's right eye and Molly's zebra-pattern collar was missing half its fur. A tuft of it was caught on Matilda's jowl.

'Thanks girls,' said Hannah, holding out her hand. 'We have to rush off now to Holborn for another screen test. A woman clairvoyant with a ghost-detecting schnauzer. There's enough mileage in the four of you to include in a series. The office will call you with the dates for all eight episodes. Shall we call for the bill?'

I didn't look at Anna. I didn't need to. I could feel her relief and excitement as we stood side by side. How on earth had we pulled this off?

'No, no, that's fine,' said Anna. 'The tea's on us.'

'We need you to email us eight different scenarios that you will be involved in over the next three months,' Hannah went on. 'Try to make them as varied as possible. When we have all the venue details, we'll send a camera crew and a director to each event.' And with that, they left.

Anna and I, always on diets, sat mesmerized and finished every item of food left on the plates in front of us. We ate as though we had been hypnotized. We even fed titbits to the dogs, who took full advantage.

'I don't think I have enough outfits for eight episodes,' said Anna, trance-like.

'We must always wear dresses,' I said. 'Let's never be seen in jeans. We want to reflect the classy side of the dog world.'

'I'm going to buy my mum a Sky package so she can watch it,' said Anna, popping scone, cream and jam into an already bulging mouth.

'I'd better call George,' I said. 'He'll be thrilled.'

They say the best part of any job is the day you are offered it. That's when you phone and tell everyone the good news. Thereafter, it's 'own up' time.

We had wanted this series ever since we'd been given a whiff of it, not for any financial gain – there wasn't any (this had been made clear) – but for the legacy. Anna was always questioning Molly's mortality, so for her, the opportunity of having a filmic record of their lives together was worth millions. For me, it was an endorsement of the radio show. The BBC had taken a risk allowing us to sabotage two hours of broadcasting every week for dogs. This TV series would validate that decision. A top reality production company had enough confidence in us to decide to include us in every episode. Now we had to come up with the ideas.

As colourful and hectic as we considered our lives to be, both of us had jobs to maintain. Filming would have to fit in with Anna's

PR company as well as *Barking at the Moon*, and I had my other radio shows. Thinking of eight different ideas was going to be tricky. The success of *Barking at the Moon* meant that our diaries were full with bookings to open and judge dog shows, but we needed to explore other activities if we were going to be varied and interesting enough to capture a TV audience.

'You can't invent activities,' said George the following night. We were in his Skoda, driving to a dinner party. 'The whole point of reality TV is that it's real. It's not manufactured to be interesting.'

'There is such a thing as dramatic licence,' I replied. 'We're simply going to explore things like swimming or cooking with the dogs – activities that might prove more entertaining than following us to the local shops and back.'

'Matilda won't like swimming,' said George. 'Man, she hates the rain. You mustn't consider swimming. And as for cooking, you don't cook and neither does Anna. It'll be obvious from the moment you turn on the oven that the two of you have no idea.'

I had learned to keep quiet when George sided with Matilda. He adored her and quite rightly missed her when she was off on a jaunt with me. This summer she was going to be away from him a great deal.

When we were in the car, she was usually asleep on the back seat, but on this night, not knowing how dog friendly the other guests would be, we had left her at home.

The dinner was in the Clapham apartment of my friend Tony. I had known him for 20 years. He was a jobbing actor and worked in fringe theatres across London. George and I always supported him by trying to see as many productions as possible.

They had got on from the moment I'd introduced them, which was quite unexpected since they were the complete antithesis of each other. George was bombastic while Tony was introverted, but both had a mutual respect for the other's talent. Tony would listen to George's late-night rants on the radio and often email the show with comments. George's respect for Tony increased even more when he discovered that it was Tony's character who had shouted the immortal lines, 'Get in the back of the van!' from the cult film *Withnail and I*. It was one of George's favourite films and he once told me that the teashop scene was filmed in the village where his family still live. He would talk about Tony on air and refer to him as 'My bleedin' talented actor mate, Tony'.

Tony's dinner parties were always a success. He was not only a great host but also a fabulous cook. This night there were six of us round the table and I knew all of them apart from an artist called Veronica. We were a noisy bunch.

Tony and his boyfriend had casseroled a pot roast in a huge enamel turine, which they placed in the middle of the table, surrounded by bowls of potatoes and fresh vegetables. George tied his napkin round his neck and clapped his hands together like an eager child.

'I love you, mate,' he said, looking at Tony with such honesty. 'Man, your dinners are bloody delicious. We always look forward to a nosh-up here.'

Everybody laughed at his enthusiasm and we started to tuck in. It was true that a cooked dinner for George and me was a novelty. We never ate meals in the flat. We both grazed and just grabbed food where and when we were hungry. I curled my toes with embarrassment as George ladled more and more food on to his plate. It was like watching somebody at an all-you-can-eat buffet.

'George, leave some for others,' I remonstrated, and then hated myself for doing so.

'It's okay,' said Tony. 'I know the size of the big fella's appetite. I always make extra.'

Incidents like this made me think of George's past. Was his ex-wife as quick to criticize as I had been? Did he eat like Neanderthal man at the dinner table because I never fed him?

George didn't let my snapping demean him. He continued to be the life and soul of the party. I felt bad for reprimanding him and made a pact with myself never to do so again. Other guests started to get fairly drunk but the two of us remained sober. I seldom drink and he drank either champagne or brandy. Since neither was usually on offer, he stuck to water.

Tony had a piano in the living room and, after the meal, most of the guests started belting out songs from musicals. I wandered into the kitchen for some more coffee and began chatting to

Veronica. She had her back to me and was stacking the sink with dirty plates.

'Is that George playing the piano?' she asked.

'I expect so,' I replied. 'It usually is.'

'He has such a talent,' she said, still with her arms in the sink. 'I've always enjoyed hearing him play.'

I took a quick breath before I responded, fearing my own question.

'Oh, do you know each other?' I asked, as calmly as I could. George had so far shown no recognition of this woman.

'Yes, he and his wife are friends of mine,' she replied. Then she turned round and we shared a look that only two women in such a conversation would share.

I wanted to ask her so many questions. How did she know them? What was his wife like? Did she know they had separated? Would she be reporting back to the wife about tonight? Would she tell her I had snapped at George's table manners? Is she younger or older than I am? Thinner or fatter? Instead, I said nothing. I went back into the front room and watched George thumping out *The Trolley Song* to a captive audience. I watched Veronica rejoin the group and marvelled at George's non-committal reaction to her. Was she winding me up? Why on earth would she do that? Not until we were in the car, on the way home, did I ask him.

'Veronica says she's a friend of yours and your wife's.'

'Yes,' he said. 'I haven't seen her for years.'

'Why didn't you tell me?' I asked.

'Tell you what? There's nothing to tell. I thought Tony must have filled you in.'

I didn't know what to say. The way he was dealing with it was so normal. Was I creating an issue that wasn't there? Again, I decided just to let it go. I had no reason to feel insecure. George demonstrated his love for me constantly, almost too much, sometimes.

When we got home, what was waiting for us drove any prospect of awkward silences well away. The moment we walked through our front door we could smell something was not right, before we saw it. Matilda was cowering in the corner, shaking, the contents of her bowels smeared across the tiny kitchen floor. Being the gentle considerate dog she is, she had confined the mess to one area. I stood, frozen, by the door.

'Wrap her in a blanket,' said George, 'and sit with her while I clean this up.'

I put her in the bath and showered her nether regions with warm water, then wrapped her in a towel and sat her on my lap. My heart was beating with panic. I'm rubbish in a crisis. George was on his hands and knees scrubbing the floor.

'Light a joss stick, and open the windows,' he said. 'We can't sleep in a room with this stench.'

'I'm driving her to the emergency, twenty-four-hour vet,' I said, my throat tight with stress. 'I'll take my car.'

George stopped scrubbing and looked at me.

'No,' he said. 'You must stop running to the vet every time she's ill. It's costing us a fortune. She has an upset tummy. It happens all the time with dogs. Heard the expression "sick as a dog"? We'll starve her for a day. She'll be okay.'

I wasn't convinced. She had stopped shaking and her breathing was steady but her head hung down and she looked pathetic. I unwrapped the towel and put her on the floor. She attempted to stand but her back legs couldn't support her. They wobbled, then gave way and she tumbled onto her side.

'That's it,' I said, grabbing my car keys. 'I'm driving her in. George, she can't even stand up.'

'No,' insisted George. 'It's not food poisoning. She hasn't been sick and she's not shaking any more. I've told you, unless blood's involved or a limb's broken, there's no need for an emergency vet. If there's no improvement in the morning, then we'll take her to our vet.'

I was caught between two thoughts. George knew far more about dogs than I did, but Anna knew more about dogs than almost anyone. As he continued to deal with the mess, I quietly went into the bathroom and called Anna. It was 1.30 a.m.

'Hello,' she answered. 'What's up?' It sounded as though she was wide awake. I couldn't believe she wasn't cross. I would have been.

'Matilda isn't well,' I told her. 'She's poohed all over the kitchen floor.'

'Oh shit,' she said, then realizing the pun, added, 'Sorry, what's she eaten?'

'Just the usual raw tripe. But you know what a scavenger she is. I'm really worried. It seems to have paralysed her. She can't stand up. George says I should stick it out till morning.'

'It's an upset tummy,' said Anna confidently. 'Bull breeds' hind legs often give way when they have gastric problems. It's the same with Molly. Don't feed her tomorrow and see what happens. George is probably right. She'll be okay in twenty-four hours.'

'Anna, I've just met a friend of his wife's,' I hissed, worried I could be heard in the rest of the tiny flat.

'What!' she exclaimed, and I could hear her lighting a cigarette. 'OMG! How did she react towards you? Did you learn anything about what he's told her?'

'She's an artist,' I whispered. 'She just said "I'm a friend of George and his wife."'

'She said I AM a friend, not I WAS a friend?' quizzed Anna.

'I know,' I conceded. 'That's what I thought. Look, I can't stay in here any longer. He'll wonder what I'm up to. Call you tomorrow.'

I came out of the bathroom to find George had wrapped Matilda in my favourite, dark brown cashmere pashmina. It would be forever covered in white fur, but as long as she recovered, I couldn't care less.

As far as Matilda's wellbeing was concerned, George was far more level-headed and calm than I could ever be, and although

I know he was fond of Anna, he found her over-emotional. Even so, if she had suggested taking Matilda to the emergency hospital, I would have done so. However highly strung her behaviour, she understood my now total maternal obsession with my dog.

George lay on the bed, Matilda next to him, and started strumming his guitar. She stared up at him. She loved music and especially guitar serenades.

'Tall and tanned and young and lovely ...' he sang, 'the girl from Ipanema goes walking ...' It was our favourite and I would always join in the word 'Ah'. By the third verse, Matilda was snoring and by morning she was hungry.

'How is the invalid?' Anna asked over the phone a few days later. Matilda and I were in the park.

'Completely recovered,' I said. 'I must learn not to panic. If it hadn't been for you and George, I would have spent the night at Elizabeth Street Hospital. I already know the name of every vet working there.'

'I was the same with Molly,' said Anna. 'You get to know what's serious and what's not after a while. Now, tell me about this friend of the wife's. Didn't you quiz George about her?'

'I tried,' I replied. 'He brushed it off. I still don't know if his wife knows about me or if we have her blessing.'

The whole episode had been playing on my mind because it was the closest I'd come to George's previous existence, when he'd lived with his family in another town. He had absorbed everything from my world, including friends and habitat. I knew nothing of the life he had known. He had a wife, two grown-up boys and a grandson. That was it. No other details. If I pushed to find out more, he would clam up.

'The only thing he has ever said to me about his family is that they're cool about it,' I said to Anna.

'I find it difficult to believe many ex-wives are cool about the new woman,' said Anna. 'But I suppose if he doesn't want to talk, you have to accept it. Nobody who knows you could ever accuse you of being a scarlet woman.'

That was the problem. Although I knew we would never be in a position to play happy families, I'd always assumed that, one day, his wife or kids, with their supposedly liberal approach to George's departure, would want to meet me. I'd imagined this would be limited to functions, such as weddings and christenings, where we would all be polite. However, having so far never been introduced to any of them, not even his older son, the likelihood seemed ever distant. We had been together for three years and George's hesitancy in discussing any of his past was unnerving me.

I heard Anna clicking the keyboard of her computer.

'Now, I've just heard back from the production company. I emailed them in the week with our list of episode ideas, and they want to film the swimming sequence next week since the weather looks good. What do you think?'

Gulp.

'Where?' I asked. 'We don't have a pool.'

'I know a guy in Highgate with one. He's a roadie friend of Y Bother's. Earns a fortune. He's always offering it to us, asking if we fancy a swim.'

'How generous,' I said. 'But would he welcome two dogs and a whole film crew? And are you back with Y Bother? If not, how can we get him to ask this guy a favour?'

Anna laughed. 'Y Bother and I still meet up from time to time,' she said. 'He told me a great joke the other night.'

'Go on,' I said.

'What do you call a drummer without a girlfriend?'

'What?'

'Homeless.'

We both burst out laughing.

'Leave it to me,' she said. 'The pool's outdoors and the roadie's got a rottweiler who swims in it.' Then she added, 'I'm not sure how Molly gets on with rottweilers, but I'm sure he's been socialized.'

'He?' I asked, imagining Molly taking on the rottie. 'Well, to be honest, I'm more concerned about the depth of the pool. Matilda enjoys wading in a stream by the South Downs, but the idea of her doing laps, way out of her depth, is a bit ambitious.'

Anna's response was, as ever, full of positivity.

'I've managed to get us a pair of award-winning Fido Float lifejackets. They cost a fortune but we have them on loan, as long as they're not damaged. If you go onto YouTube, you'll see bull breeds wearing them for surfing, swimming and hydrotherapy. Swimming is a very therapeutic activity for dogs.'

I was watching Matilda lying in the sun, snoring.

'Matilda's lifejacket is orange and has a handle, so that you can support her and never let her go,' Anna continued. I relaxed a little.

'You're right,' I said. 'It will do her limbs the world of good. And my thighs. A little cellulite prevention. I'll come over and collect it.'

'No need,' said Anna. 'I've couriered it over.'

Oh Lord! Matilda and I ran as fast as her little legs would go, back to the flat. We arrived just in time to see the motorbike courier getting back on his bike and when I opened the front door, the scene I'd dreaded was in full flow. George was holding the attractive orange lifejacket, fresh from it's wrapping.

'Is this some sort of corset?' he asked, expectantly. 'It's just arrived.'

'Don't be silly,' I sighed. 'Since when have I indulged in mail-order underwear? It's a lifejacket for Matilda.'

'So you *are* taking her swimming,' he said. 'She won't like it.'

'We don't know she won't like it,' I replied. 'Bulldogs are often advised to swim for mobility reasons. And if she doesn't look as though she wants to go in, I won't make her.'

George knelt down and patted Matilda, who, as usual, was looking up at him adoringly.

'Let's try the jacket on,' I said. 'If she doesn't like it, we'll take it off and that's an end to it.'

George watched while I fitted the jacket on to Matilda and did up all the safety buckles. Bulldogs are known for their humour, and often enjoy dressing up. She stood quite content in the jacket, not pulling it or attempting to get out of it. She just stared at me as if to say, 'Now what?'

'Promise me you'll take her out if she looks as though she isn't enjoying it,' George said, picking up his guitar. He lay on the bed and serenaded us with *My Girl*.

Having fitted the girls out in swimwear, Anna and I were in a panic about what to wear ourselves. She could have got away with a bikini, but I couldn't, and I was damned if she was going to upstage me!

'Pretty one-piece costumes,' I suggested. 'But nothing that will detract from the dogs.'

'I agree,' said Anna. 'I have a jazzy number Y Bother chose for me in Bali a few years back. I don't think I've worn it since, but my weight's about the same. I'm more worried about my legs. They're going to be filming underwater, apparently, and my legs are very white.'

'What!' I screamed. 'Underwater! Oh Lord, we must book waxes immediately. Imagine a close-up of Molly's dog paddle and your bikini line in full view!'

Anna and I are both proud of our legs. Unlike the rest of our bodies, we have the legs of teenagers – probably down to a passion for yoga. If the film crew were to capture any part of our bodies, the legs were perhaps the best bits.

'Let's apply fake tan the night before,' suggested Anna. 'I have some waterproof stuff left over from last summer.'

The day of the swimming episode, as it had become known, started brightly enough. Anna and I were to arrive at the private north London pool after the crew – two cameramen, one of whom was to take the underwater shots, a director and his researcher and a sound guy. They were all dressed in shorts, obviously well prepared. From the moment we pulled up in the mini, they would start filming. No preamble. This was reality. George was right. We may have found the venue, but from the moment the camera turned, we were on our own.

Anna knew the owner of the pool, but not his rottweiler, Charlie. Neither of us had ever set foot in his home or, until now, seen the pool.

We were shown in by a maid, who directed all of us through to the garden and then closed the patio doors. The message was pretty much, 'Do whatever you want outside but don't come dripping back into the house.'

We stopped to take in our surroundings. The crew had set up down one end of the pool near the house. It was a large pool, surrounded by summer garden furniture and overhung by trees and shrubbery – very secluded and very luxurious. Drummers must earn a whack. Of the owner there was no sign, but Charlie was standing on a float in the middle of the pool, big, well balanced and majestic. On seeing us, he somehow managed to propel the float over, like an intrepid explorer. The camera followed the action while the two production crew watched on a portable monitor set up on a garden table. The sound man held a mic, strapped to a long pole over the pool.

Anna's antennae were out, clocking how Molly and Charlie reacted to each other. She was holding every dog-friendly swimming product she had ever marketed under one arm and Molly's lead in the other. I held our costumes and towels and Matilda, and was casting around for somewhere to change. There were no outbuildings.

'Look,' I cried, nodding towards some rhododendron bushes. 'Let's get changed behind those.' The camera began to move forwards. Anna was aghast.

'Outdoors? Getting changed outdoors? Oh blimey!'

We tied the dogs to a large table, complete with sun parasol, and crept into the foliage. There is something very British about getting changed outdoors, trying to shield your bare bottom from view, whether it's at the seaside or scrabbling about in a private herbaceous border. Having squeezed myself into my new floral costume, I decided to leave my clothes where they were, and stepped out from behind the foliage. Quite concerned about my streaky, obviously fake tan, I did a little frivolous skip for the camera and went to fit Matilda with her lifejacket, all the while holding my stomach in.

'Have you seen my knickers?' Anna's concerned call came from the end of the garden. After a great deal of foliage rustling, she appeared, in her jazzy one piece, creeping backwards into vision, looking for all the world like a Dick Emery character. Turning round, she announced to all of us, 'I've lost some of my underwear.'

'That's the least of your problems,' I thought. One of her breasts was completely exposed. The swimming costume may have fitted in Bali but it certainly didn't come close to it in Highgate.

By now, Charlie had leapt from his floating platform and was back on dry land. He shook his massive, wet body, drenching all of us, including the crew, then started barking at Molly and Matilda. He was commanding them to play by running up and down the edge of the pool, in circles. We decided to ignore him.

The Fido Float lifejackets fitted the girls beautifully. Molly was in day-glo green and Matilda in Buddhist orange. All four of us stood timidly by the steps leading into the pool. The cameraman, recording every second, was on the other side. The underwater cameraman sat and waited. Anna chose one of her water-friendly dog toys, the Pushy Poisson – a fish-shaped chew – and threw it to land a few feet from Charlie. He stopped barking and went to retrieve it.

'That should distract him,' she said, lifting up Molly, who looked calmly at the pool as Anna stood on the first step with just her feet in the water. I picked up hefty Matilda and followed suit. Matilda froze. She didn't struggle. She trusted me.

'How often has Molly been in a pool?' I asked, genuinely interested. The camera moved in closer. Anna gave me a look of disbelief.

'Umm ... well, not that often,' she said. 'Okay Molls, one step at a time.'

Oh my God. We were in the same boat. We were subjecting our dogs to social swimming when neither of them had ever experienced it before. Would we ever have enticed them into a pool if there had been no camera? Our casual trips to the seaside had included both dogs running in and out of the waves, but immersion in a heated pool was somewhat different. George's words kept drifting into my head – 'She won't like it. She has never shown any inclination for swimming.' I looked down at Matilda in her orange lifejacket. She enjoyed being carried, so appeared quite calm.

Our favourite photo – two rock chicks photographed by the rock
legend himself, Bryan Adams

Working off an 'Honest Sausage' in Regent's Park

only as good as its research!

Bonjour! Two bitches and their two bitches à Paris.

In 'dogue' it's all about the accessories.

A passport pict[...]
a thousand wor[...]

Anna before her emotional meltdown at the grave of Rin Tin Tin.

Twelve legs set forth to the Eiffel Tower — but first some retail therapy.

Happy days ... Jo and Big George.

Tickled pink and looking sharp, Big George out with his girl in Soho.

Cooling off in a wet T-shirt – the dogs not us!

Buttons and bows: Mabel at twelve weeks.

Do our bums look big in this?

With the master of double entendre –
Julian Clary.

Four Sugar Plum Fairies at the
sky picnic.

Getting down with the dogs. Woof! Woof!

Macy Gray trying to look as short as us!

THE BRITISH
BROADCASTING CORPORATION

Why no signs dogs allowed?

Cake made in the image of our beloveds.

Knit your own pet. We did!

We only sit here if the bath is empty.

Anna was now standing up to her waist and was about to float Molly onto the water while still holding the lifejacket handle. Molly struggled a little. Anna lent towards her, away from the camera, and began talking to her in their own language. As usual, Molly listened.

'Now come on little noo doin what Ma does the swimming and the grinning.' Molly licked Anna's face. The sound guy, leaning over the pool, held the mic over their heads. 'Let's sing the swimming song, Molly Moo,' said Anna encouragingly.

With that, she gently raised Molly into the air, all the time holding on to her jacket handle, and started singing.

'Molly does her swimming, Molly does her swimming ... merrily, merrily, Molly does her swimming.'

'That's the same bloody tune as the noodle song,' I thought, but it did the trick. Molly, still being held in the air, started doing swimming strokes, like an ariel ballet. She was doing cycling actions, literally in the air. With no sense of panic, Anna lowered and glided her into the water, where she started to do dog paddle.

'Yay,' said Anna. 'Good girl, Molls, good girl.' Molly, with her head held high above the water – like my mum when she's doing breaststroke – allowed Anna, now out of her depth, to steer her into the centre of the pool. The two of them were swimming side by side. They looked very at ease.

'Right, come on Matilda,' I said, carefully going down the steps and into the water until it came up to my waist. 'Let's see what you can do.'

Matilda is a dead weight. She is not as lithe as Molly and her legs are much shorter. Holding onto the jacket handle, I lowered her into the water. Her jowls floated on the surface. My concern was to avoid getting water into her nose. Bulldogs are not known for good breathing and at no cost should she go under.

'Look,' I shouted. 'She's swimming!'

Matilda, eager to join her friend Molly, paddled towards the middle of the pool as I held her. I began to feel very emotional. I remembered when my father had taught me to swim as a very young child, and the moment he led me into the deep end and I paddled to stay afloat. That was years ago. Now Molly and Matilda were doing the same, paddling their little legs while we held them by the handle of their lifejackets.

'I'm so proud of them,' said Anna, turning to me, and I knew how she felt.

For owners of labradors, collies or natural water-loving breeds, a dog swimming is no big deal. How many times do you see one running amok in a London park, jumping into ponds out of pure desire? For bull breeds, though, especially flat-nosed dogs, this was a big step forward. We would never risk taking them into water so deep without lifejackets, but for exercise, swimming is difficult to beat.

'Watch out!'

The peace in the pool was broken by a shout from the director to the sound man, who was still leaning over the pool with his extended mic. Crashing out from behind the shrubbery came Charlie, knocking over the table with the parasol, barking and bolting at the same time. Gone was the Pushy Poisson, replaced by something white and flimsy. Up and down he raced, around the edge of the pool. He seemed to be goading us, barking and throwing the white item in the air and then catching it. The sound man and crew followed all his antics while the director stared at the monitor.

'He's got my knickers,' shouted Anna. 'How the hell did he find those?'

Molly and Matilda, sensing a crisis, both headed towards the steps out of the pool, their little legs going like engines. Anna and I swam alongside them, still holding them, trying to keep up and not panic.

SPLASH!

Charlie had dive-bombed into the centre of the pool, making a massive wave and throwing water all over the spectators as well as creating a strong current around the four of us. My main concern was that Matilda's nose did not go under. I held her as high as I could above my head as the current pulled me down and I found myself looking straight into the lens of the underwater camera, held by the kitted-out cameraman. I remember seeing Anna's well-waxed legs moving frog-like through the water, Molly's four little legs paddling fast ahead of her. Gravity pulled me back up to the surface, gasping for air and desperate to take a look at Matilda. I could still only move one arm, the other was firmly round her lifejacket. Her head was dry and she was intent on reaching the shallow end of the pool. Anna and Molly were already on the poolside. I handed Matilda up, pulled myself out and sat panting on the edge.

I couldn't speak, I was so in shock. Anna was drying Molly, who was unperturbed by events, and Matilda, after shaking herself, ran to claim ownership of the abandoned Pushy Poisson. The film crew kept filming. Nobody, apart from me, seemed to be concerned. Everything was normal. The poem I'd learned at college, 'Not waving but drowning', sprung to my mind.

Charlie, master of all he surveyed, was back on his floating platform, the knickers over one ear. The hand-held mic was on the pole over his head, picking up the lapping sound of his float.

'Get a shot of the pants,' shouted the director. 'A gusset shot, we need a close-up on the gusset.'

I lent in towards Anna, who was now dressing Molly in a nice warm fleece. The two of us were obviously not on mic. I could see that she, like me, was shaking.

'Anna, I almost ...' I started.

'I know,' she whispered, finishing my sentence for me. 'I'm keeping calm for the dogs. Let's talk about it later.'

'Right,' called the director from the other end. 'Let's film one dog at a time in a "sit" so that we can do a voice-over for each of them, and then Anna and Jo, can we have you both in deckchairs for an interview?'

Each dog sat, individually, for two minutes while the camera filmed them. Their designated voices would be added later in the edit, recording their supposed thoughts on the morning. Charlie's voice, we were told, was to have a strong German accent.

Then it was Anna's and my turn. Without any make-up, hair wet and tans streaked, we were asked, in close-up, our thoughts on the morning. Knowing how unattractive I must look and bowing to Anna's greater knowledge on the swimming benefits for dogs, I let her do the talking. To everyone else, the morning had passed without incident. The crew got their footage and our dogs got their exercise. Charlie had had a couple of mates round for a swim and by the time the roadie returned home, the pool was all put back to normal.

Anna and I knew, however, how close we had been to things turning out differently. Our journey home in the Union Jack mini was far more sombre than our journey earlier. Maybe the two of us were feeling slightly emabarrassed at our willingness to thrust ourselves, as well as our dogs, into the limelight.

'I will never, ever jeopardize Molly's health or life,' said Anna as we sat in traffic on Highgate Hill.

'I know that,' I said. 'Nor me Matilda's, and I don't think we ever have.'

'And we never must,' added Anna. 'Not for anyone or anything.'

'No,' I agreed.

We drove in silence, thinking our own thoughts, the dogs, exhausted, asleep on the back seat. There were seven more episodes to film. Would they all be as stressful as this? What had we got ourselves into?

George was waiting when we got home. He was lying on the bed, playing the guitar, and next to him was a plate of half-eaten sponge cake. Matilda wiggled her bottom and waited for him to lift her up.

'Well that went well,' I said brightly.

He looked at me as he continued strumming, the way guitar players do.

'Matilda seemed to love it,' I said. 'She took to it like a duck to water.'

He stopped playing and lay the guitar down.

'She would,' he said, looking straight into my eyes. 'Because that's what dogs do. They never want to let you down.'

I went into the bathroom, turned on the taps and burst into tears.

CHAPTER 4

'Time is right and we're moving on.'

'It's the Debbie Harry concert tonight,' Anna enthused. We were sitting in traffic on the Tottenham Court Road.

'At last,' I grinned. 'You've been banging on about it for days.'

'What do you think of the hair?' she asked, turning her head from side to side. 'I had my re-growth done yesterday. Oh, and take a look on the back seat.'

I peered round and, there, displayed between the neatly seat-belted Molly and Matilda, was a brand new pair of cerise cowboy boots. She must have slipped them in after I'd put Matilda in the car.

'Very Blondie,' I said. 'What time do you need to be there?'

'Seven o'clock, Café de Paris,' she said. 'Y Bother's going to meet me outside.'

'What a clever bloke,' I thought. In what must have been his final desperate attempt to win back Anna's affections, he had managed to blag press tickets for her all-time favourite singer. It was even rumoured that some of the original band would be performing with her. I'd not seen Anna this excited since Molly had executed her first somersault. She had spent days shopping for the perfect pair of skinny jeans with matching maroon leather jacket, and *Heart of Glass* had become the soundtrack to her life.

'Time is right and I'm moving on, I'm going to be your number one.'

Debbie's somewhat raunchy tones were blasting out of the car stereo as we turned into Soho Square.

'She has a Japanese chin,' Anna said, tapping her fingers on the steering wheel.

'That's not very nice,' I said. 'Couldn't she get it done?'

'No, I mean Debbie Harry's dog. It's a Japanese chin.'

Sometimes I wonder if Anna would have time for anyone, even her pop idol, if they didn't show an interest in dogs. Personally, I was never a fan of Blondie's, and aside from the three of us all sharing the 'fair and fading' label, I couldn't see the appeal.

Anna, on the other hand, had been to most of the band's London concerts and was looking forward to Debbie's come-back in this smaller, more intimate venue. She'd not mentioned Y Bother for weeks but it seemed this treat had placed him back in her good books.

'George is seeing the doctor for a check-up today,' I said, turning the music down a bit.

'Really?' she replied. 'I'm a bit worried about Molly, actually, and the number of times she wees.'

'George won't tell me his concerns. He says he just wants to get checked out,' I answered. Then added, 'What do you mean, the number of times she wees? She wees the same as Matilda.'

'She often can't go through the night,' Anna replied.

'Neither can I,' I said. 'It's age. Molly's knocking on a bit.' I looked out of my passenger window. 'Are we here? Where's this studio?'

Anna checked her sat nav, indicated and pulled over.

'This should be it,' she said. 'They said they had reserved a parking place for us right outside.'

We were in a tiny street off Soho Square, outside the offices of a large advertising agency. Surprisingly, given the London traffic, we had managed to arrive right on time. This was the first engagement we had been offered as a direct result of our radio show. Maybe 'engagement' is the wrong word, because that denotes payment. No money was changing hands for this booking. We had been asked to join a campaign to raise awareness of lungworm, and had been told to think of it as more of an honour than an earner. The offer had arrived by email, turning Anna almost hysterical.

'Do you know how bad lungworm can be?' she screeched at me, clapping her hands.

'No,' I answered.

'Oh my God,' she cried. 'Lungworm is also known as *Angiostrongylus vasorum* or French heartworm. It's a nasty parasite that can kill dogs. If ingested, the "worm" actually goes straight for the heart. The parasite lives on slugs and if a dog accidentally eats an infected slug, the dog will die unless treated quickly. Its heart will be eaten away.'

She was standing, staring at me, hunched and impassioned, like a blonde Edith Piaf.

'Please tell me you've only just learned all that,' I said.

'Oh no,' she answered. 'Molly and I have lived under the cloud of lungworm since we acquired a bigger garden. The thought of it often keeps me awake at night.'

I was beginning to see how vital our part in this fight against the killer worm was.

The ad agency had asked for the four of us to contribute to an online, looped interview with one of the country's top TV vets, Luke Gamble. Our BBC station would also stream the live, internet podcast with Molly and Matilda. It was hoped that the session would educate dog owners on how best to avoid the parasite.

As we approached the agency's front door, Anna tried to coax Molly.

'Pants, pants,' she urged. 'She's done two wees but as yet no pants.'

'Well, maybe a lengthy discussion on a killer parasite will help move her bowels,' I said, pressing the buzzer.

Why are ad agency people so trendy? Two model-type young girls tottered out from behind reception, fell to their knees at the sight of our dogs and then gestured us vaguely towards a spiral staircase and the studios below. What should have been a simple descent became a major obstacle course. The staircase was ridiculously groovy, made up of tiny mesh-like holes. The moment we approached it, both dogs instinctively recoiled in fear, sensing that this wasn't solid ground. It was a bit like expecting them to walk over a cattle grid.

With some force, we managed to coerce them onto the first step, at the same time as our stilettos got stuck in the little holes. Both of us were proudly wearing our new Diane Von Furstenberg wrap-around dresses, in an attempt to put style back into the dog world. As we stumbled and cursed our way down the tiny spiral staircase, we glimpsed, through the mesh, the welcoming committee below. Silently awaiting our landing and doing their best not to look up our dresses were the producer, the engineer, the ad men and the client.

Eventually, the four of us reached the bottom, and after unravelling tangled dog leads and sashes from wrap-around dresses, there was a lot of hand-shaking and patting of dogs.

'Now, ladies,' said the man from the ad agency, 'we're going to take you down to the studio where you will meet the vet, Luke Gamble. You can have a little chat with him, then we'll mic you up and if you could give us about an hour, that would be great.'

'An hour?' I asked. 'To do what?'

'Talk about lungworm,' he answered, smiling.

'Is there an hour's worth of content in lungworm?' I asked. 'It seems like a long time.'

'Oh my God, yes,' butted in Anna, ebullient at the thought. 'It's a massive subject. For example, we can discuss signs to look out for, such as strange coughing, loss of weight, loss of energy and difficulty breathing.' She paused for a moment, distracted. 'But I'm worried that Molly hasn't done a pants and the thought of her in a hot studio for an hour ...'

'I could always take her out for a walk if she seems in need,' suggested the kindly engineer.

Anna, who would rather run naked down Baker Street than have anyone else in charge of Molly, including me, smiled at the engineer.

'It's okay, thanks,' she said hurriedly. 'I've packed a "Keep Fido as Cool as a Cucumber" collar. I'll slip that on her if she starts to overheat.'

The studio was at the end of a long corridor and we were invited to wait, alone, on a plush velvet sofa, in the corridor, while the red light was on. Apparently, Luke was winding up a previous interview for breakfast television. On the table in front of us was a selection of kiwi fruit and croissants.

'I've always quite fancied him,' said Anna. 'I think he has the most integrity of all the TV vets.'

'I'm not sure which one he is,' I said. 'He's not the guy who wanders around in the blue pyjamas operating garb?'

'Oh no,' she said. 'Luke wears shorts. At least, he does on the telly. Might be a bit chilly for him on a day like this. They say it might snow.'

I shifted a little on the sofa and dropped a slice of kiwi into Matilda's eager and dribbling mouth.

George would have found all of this very amusing. So much chic and showbiz surrounding canine ailments. Was he, I wondered, now at the doctor's? I had no idea what time his appointment was. The mention of a medical had come as a complete surprise. It was common knowledge that he had suffered a massive heart attack well over ten years earlier due to work overload. But he boasted to all and sundry that his wife had nursed him back to health and that, with a complete rethink of diet and lifestyle, he was now the fittest he had ever been.

'I'm healthier than most men of my age,' he would tell me as well as the listeners. 'The heart is a muscle and mine is now twice as strong.'

He was so large and capable I had no reason not to believe him, and I would drag him to dynamic yoga classes both in London and New York, where he showed as much stamina, if not more, than any other student. Only once did I quiz him, when we were about to board a long-haul flight to the US.

'What should I do if you have a heart attack in the air?'

'Leave me,' he said. 'Just leave me.'

And then we laughed at how dismissive he was of his life.

Maybe the medical had nothing to do with his heart. It could be that he simply wanted to have an MOT, although the very idea was completely out of character. He had never registered with a doctor in London, which made the decision even more odd. That morning, as Matilda and I were on our way out for the day – I had just opened the front door – George's voice halted us.

'I'm rocking into one of those walk-in private medical clinics in Harley Street,' he called from the bathroom. 'Just to get the once over.'

That stopped me in my tracks.

'Why? Don't you feel okay? What's up?' I almost snapped.

'Nothing's up,' he said, appearing at the door with my moisturizer all over his face. 'It's just they're doin' a deal at the moment. They've got advertisements in the window. A hundred pounds to walk in and walk out in thirty minutes. Thought I'd give it a go.'

He spoke as though he was finding stuff to fill his day.

'George, what's this about?' I was beginning to stress out. 'What do you mean you'll "give it a go"? What's wrong with you?'

'Don't shout at me,' he said, shouting. 'See. I knew I shouldn't have told you. Nothing's wrong with me. It's just they're doin' an offer.'

'Don't be silly,' I screamed. 'An offer? This is a doctor. It's your health we're talking about, not loyalty points!'

'Stop screaming, you'll upset Matilda,' he said through gritted teeth. 'I'm just popping in for a check-up. Now let it go.'

Sitting two floors below ground and munching on an all-butter croissant, I racked my brain trying to recall any recent clues that could have been significant concerning his health. I was surprised he hadn't sent me a picture of the waiting room by now. I glanced at my phone and realized there was no signal, so if he was texting, I wouldn't know.

At that moment the red studio light went off and an engineer emerged from the gallery.

'Jo and Anna, this way please,' he said, and we were ushered into the tiny studio. 'Luke, let me introduce you to the Barking Blondes.'

Seated on the sofa, all ready for the marathon session on lung-worm, was Luke Gamble. In shorts. He was very attractive in an outdoor, pioneering, boy scout sort of way. Anna certainly seemed to think so. She almost curtsied on sight and thrust Molly forward as though they had been granted an audience with the Pope.

'This is Molly,' she said. 'Ten years old, but I'm told the teeth of a two year old.'

Luke looked impressed. He stood up to shake our hands, then sat down again. His shorts had ridden up a little.

'How are we going to play this?' he asked, as the engineer clipped mics on to all of us. Then, after some thought, he added, 'I suggest you ask me questions and I'll just keep talking. I'm told this is being streamed live online. How long is this slot, have you any idea?'

'An hour,' I said.

'Blimey,' he answered. 'Well, I suppose there's enough information to fill an hour.'

'Oh yes,' agreed Anna, dreamily. 'Once we get on to the subject of fox poo, the minutes will fly by.'

Molly and Matilda lay obediently at Luke's feet. Anna looked at them both enviously, then, on the signal, she launched into it.

'Luke, tell us about lungworm? What is it exactly?'

The two of them had judged correctly. There seemed to be loads to say. The questions and answers just kept coming. Luke and Anna joyously indulged in the exploration of this killer parasite while I sat and listened and nodded and wondered who on earth was watching this? Were there people in offices, all over the country, surreptitiously tuning in to a lungworm debate?

As engrossed as they both were, I couldn't help feeling I was witnessing some sort of online canine debating foreplay. Anna couldn't take her eyes off Luke's large red safari legs in his khaki shorts. I doubt even Molly's panting would have distracted her.

'Luke' – she was now in full command – 'is it true that foxes propagate the parasite through their poo – slugs slide on to the poo, the parasite attaches itself to them and lays its eggs on the slugs?'

'Absolutely, Anna. This is why we must be so careful when taking our dogs into London parks ...'

I looked at the dogs. Then I spotted the engineer through the studio window, seated at his mixing desk. He was reading a newspaper and eating a doughnut. Maybe he didn't have a dog, or maybe the whole topic left him queasy so he'd turned the sound down.

Silence.

I suddenly realized that nobody was talking and both sets of eyes were directed expectantly towards me.

'Interesting,' I said, feigning curiosity in an attempt to fill a few more precious minutes. 'And how can we treat lungworm?'

'Well, ...' began Luke, and I settled back into my thoughts again, watching the khaki shorts getting ever shorter.

For Anna, I guess the time really did fly since she was enjoying herself. For me, 60 minutes of lungworm palled somewhat and by the time we were released from the clammy studio, I was almost hyperventilating. Luke was charming, and as we shook hands, Anna thrust one of our newly designed *Barking at the Moon* business cards at him.

'You must come on to our radio show one evening,' she cooed.

I wondered if he wore long trousers at night.

'Would love to,' he said. 'Bit tricky getting back into London in the evening, though. My wife and I have a smallholding out in the country.'

Without a flicker, Anna, clever girl, kept her smile going.

'Well, any Thursday you can get away we would love to have you on air with us. Woof! Woof!'

With that, we turned to make our ungainly ascent back up the staircase. An engineer was lingering by the front door. When we appeared he stepped, apologetically, towards us.

'There was a bit of a problem with that streaming, the BBC end,' he muttered.

We stared at him in disbelief.

'They weren't answering my calls,' he admitted, sheepishly. 'So I'm afraid they haven't taken it from us. Think it must have been a glitch.'

What?

'Luke's lot are okay, though,' he continued. 'They'll be able to use some of it.'

He scurried back down the ridiculous staircase.

We waited until we were outside, and watching Molly squat, before we erupted.

'I've just endured an hour of lungworm, squashed into a tiny underground room with a vet in a pair of shrinking shorts, and *none* of the footage was delivered to the place it was intended?!' I screeched.

Anna slowly shook her head. 'We'd given them the wrong ISDN number. I don't believe it. I thought we had an exclusive for them. Never mind, Luke was saying that we may be used on the posters.'

'Well, let's not hold our breath on that one,' I said, feeling deflated. 'Let's have coffee and share a cake. I need a sugar boost.'

We crossed the road to a cheery-looking greasy spoon opposite. It was obvious that dogs were allowed because, as we went in, I noticed a rottweiler asleep under a table. Seated, above him, were a couple enjoying full English breakfasts.

The woman looked up as we led Molly and Matilda to the table next to them. Their dog didn't stir, but she continued to stare at the four of us. Her arms and neck were covered in a tattoo of a rottweiler and a line of studs adorned her nose. The bloke was tattooed across his bald head with what looked like a German shepherd dog, and he was mopping up egg yolk with a saveloy.

'Oh Lord, my Diane Von Furstenberg is going to reek of fried food after being in here,' said Anna. Then she spotted the rottweiler and bristled.

'Molly gruffal, nood gruffal.'

The rottweiler slept on, not bothering to move.

Ding! Ding! Ding! Ding! Now that we had come back above ground, texts were arriving in quick succession. The tattooed woman, her mouth full of bacon, put down her fork, a look of realization spreading across her bulging face.

'Bloody hell,' she said, when she was able to speak. 'It's you two, isn't it? You're the mad dog women? Off the wireless. Oh my God! Woof! Woof!'

She stood up and walked over to us. At the same time, her rottweiler, who was tied to the table, woke up and followed, dragging the table with him.

'I love you two,' she said, sitting down on a spare chair at our table. 'I bleedin' love you. Look, Barry, this bulldog's got a bow tie. Bloody hell! What you doin' in this neck of the woods?'

'Oh, an important junket on canine disease,' Anna said, grabbing Molly's collar. Her radar was now on full alert. She stood up and placed herself between the rottie and Molly.

'Gruffal, Molls, gruffal,' she said under her breath, patting Molly's head.

'Oh, you're using your language,' shouted the woman. 'Barry, come here and listen to this. This dog and Anna here can sing in harmony with one another. Go on ... do a bit for Barry.'

A workman who had been reading his paper at a corner table looked up expectantly. The proprietor and his son came round from behind the counter, drying their hands, and stood waiting. Could this day get any worse?

'Actually, Molly's a bit tired,' said Anna, clocking my despair. 'She's just assisted in a debate on lungworm. If you don't mind, I'd rather she rested.'

Another text arrived on my phone.

'Excuse me,' I said and started to read the message. The woman retreated, disappointed, back to Barry and his breakfast.

I went through my texts. Harrods were expecting us at two that afternoon to open their new Pet Spa. It had been in the diary for some time and involved quite a lot of organizing. Our dogs were required to show full vaccination papers before they could be allowed in. This was our second big booking due to the radio show, and again no fee. However, there was enormous prestige in being photographed opening a pet department in 'The Top People's Store'. Patrick Cox, the designer, and owner of two bull-dogs, was opening the spa with us and we were all expected to arrive at the same time.

Back in the mini, heading towards Knightsbridge, smelling of fried food and with Debbie Harry on the stereo, we were all in a better mood. Maybe it was Anna's excitement at the thought of that night's concert or just the sheer pleasure of travelling with our dogs but the four of us sped round Hyde Park Corner like a mobile disco. Molly barked the chorus and we joined in on full throttle.

'I'm not the kind of girl who gives up just like that. Time is right and we're moving on, we're going to be your number one...!'

Molly loved communal singing and the noise was so loud, even with the windows up, that people pulling up alongside at the traffic lights looked at us and burst out laughing.

My phone started to ring. It was George. I turned the music down.

'Watcha,' he said. 'Where are you?'

'On the way to Harrods,' I said. 'Remember? We're opening the Pet Spa.'

'How's Matilda?' he asked. 'I feel I never see her.'

'She's listening to Blondie,' I said. 'We all are. Anna's going to see her live tonight at the Café de Paris.'

'I know her drummer,' said George. 'Top bloke. Kept fish. Listen, don't let them do anything crazy to Matilda, will you? Like nail varnish or hair spray or anything, will you? Tarting her up. That sort of girlie stuff. She won't like it.'

Alarm bells started to ring. I had my suspicions that most of the above treatments were on the menu. This was the luxury market.

'George, I would never let anything happen to Matilda that she didn't enjoy,' I said. 'Look, we've got to go. We've just arrived and a doorman is directing us to the car park.'

'Any chance I can ...?' he started to ask. But I'd hung up. I knew he wanted to see Matilda, but the day was running away with us and there was still loads to fit in.

'How is he?' said Anna. 'What happened at the medical?'

'I didn't ask,' I admitted. But then again, he hadn't offered me the information. 'I'll find out later,' I said as we handed over the car keys to a green-suited attendant. 'We have to get through this afternoon first.'

From nowhere, another uniformed assistant appeared by our side. He led us to the entrance and, with a flourish, held open the main door to the store.

Anyone who has walked through the pet department of Harrods will know that it is the height of decadence, offering merchandise that befits its opulent and wealthy clientele. Diamond-encrusted collars, luxury prams, designer outfits – it's all there in abundance. At the rear, a food counter sells doggy cup cakes and pawfiteroles, more proof of a thriving market aimed at owners who will spend anything on their pets.

A Different Breed had filmed an episode with the four of us in the doggy clothing department a few weeks earlier. We were shopping for fancy-dress outfits and had chosen a ladybird costume for Molly and a hippopotamus for Matilda. The crew had found Matilda's face encased in comedy hippo mouth very amusing, and she seemed to love it, but once we got back home, I never took it out of its bag. I'd thrown it in the back of the cupboard, out of George's sight, where it remained in the identifiable green bag. So we were familiar with the impressive department's layout. Now they were opening the long-awaited spa.

Another green-uniformed assistant, complete with headset, accompanied us towards the VIP lift. By now, even in Harrods, our dogs had attracted a lot of attention, and shoppers crowded round to see what was happening. Holding the group of spectators back, the assistant ushered us into the lift and we headed up to the top floor. As the lift doors sprung open, we were revealed to a large group of waiting press, a welcoming committee and a small number of hand-picked, fashionable customers.

Patrick Cox and his handsome bulldog, Caesar, joined us for the photo call and the grand cutting of the ribbon to declare the spa open. Then there were more photos and as Molly and Matilda were being placed in line and fussed over by the photographers, I caught Anna's eye.

'Is this really happening?' she giggled.

I understood her mood completely. The whole day was a result of a weekly radio show about dogs. We were becoming, in the dog world, VIPs and treated as such. There had been times in the past when I was too scared to walk into Harrods for fear of wearing the wrong jeans, whereas now they had valet-parked our car, given us a bodyguard and thrust a glass of champagne into our hands.

Our dogs, on the other hand, could have been anywhere. We lapped up the luxury but, for them, being at the top store in Knightsbridge was no different from being in a backyard in Hackney, as long as we were with them.

Anna, however, had always emphasized the importance of mental stimulation. 'Keep your dog's mind agile by feeding her as many different experiences as possible,' she would say. 'It helps her to remain young and alert.'

Well, our two had social calendars even Nigel Dempster, the celebrated gossip columnist, would have envied. What was becoming more apparent, amid all this excitement, was that Anna and I were being forced to trust our instincts about where to draw the line, when to indulge and when to admit enough was enough. It was agreed that the moment either dog appeared stressed or uncomfortable in any environment, we would remove them. So far, they seemed to find it all as much of an adventure as the two of us did.

Before leaving, we were invited to take a guided tour and pamper the girls with some complimentary treatments. There were five or six consulting rooms, each staffed by white-coated beauticians and therapists, ready to pamper four-legged clients. Included in the standard grooming treatments offered were pawdicures, skin packs, blow-dries and massage.

In one room, Caesar was having his nails painted silver while being blow dried by a young Polish girl. Anna couldn't have been more excited about Molly's blueberry, therapeutic mask than if it had been applied on herself.

I was hesitant over accepting any treatments for Matilda. George's guarded advice kept going round my head and I knew what his reaction would be if he set foot in the place. This was the man who made a dog toy out of one of his socks, and flinched when I paid over £50 for a collar.

Finally, I chose a deep-tissue, sea-clay wrap, which I thought would benefit her joints and, unlike silver nail varnish, would keep all evidence hidden.

Both dogs were wrapped in aluminium foil for ten minutes to allow the treatments to sink in. Next they were rinsed off and left to sleep. The process seemed to have been beneficial – they lay in front of us, chilled and snoring. Enya floated out of surround-sound speakers.

Anna and I relaxed on padded loungers, sipping herbal teas, and talked about the night ahead.

'I'm going straight back for a bath-bomb soak,' said Anna. 'Then I'll put on my glad rags and treat myself to a cab to Piccadilly. Y Bother says we can eat there, at the Café de Paris.'

'Okay, I'll text George to come and pick us up, I said. 'You can scoot straight off without having to drop us back home.'

'Will he do that?' asked Anna. 'It's rush hour and he's got to drive through the centre of London.'

'He enjoys it,' I said. 'George's dream would be to drive us everywhere in his Skoda and act as bodyguard.'

'I think the days of us being mobbed are fast approaching, especially once the lungworm poster is out!' laughed Anna, just as the manager of the spa approached.

He stood politely by our side, lent forward and said, 'We would be honoured if Molly and Matilda would leave their footprints in the Harrods Pet Spa Walk of Fame. You will find the designated area just by the entrance.'

Anna was off the lounger and waking Molly up before you could shout Marilyn Monroe!

'Quick, Molls,' she said, grabbing the lead and accompanying the manager to the spa entrance. I followed with a much more belligerent Matilda. After her relaxing mudpack, she wanted nothing more than to continue her long snooze.

Some uninvited shoppers were watching from behind the barrier, along with a couple of press people. Patrick Cox was on his hands and knees, gently placing Caesar's paws on to a patch of wet concrete. As yet, there were no other paw prints. The crowd gave a round of applause. The moment he stood up and dusted down his cashmere trousers and led his dog away, Anna was kneeling down, Molly poised by her side.

'I'm going to angle her right paw so that her corn won't come out in the imprint,' Anna told the onlookers. I was beginning to wish I'd worn slacks. In order for Molly's paw prints to be placed in the middle of the wet concrete – in other words, more prominently – Anna had to lift her up and lean over. Molly, as always, calmly accepted this and allowed her left paw to be placed down and then lifted up. It was the perfect little miniature bull terrier print. The crowd clapped. Anna lent in to place the right paw, corn side up. At that moment, something fell out of Anna's bra and landed splat in the wet concrete. It looked for all the world like a Swedish meatball. Nobody moved and nobody clapped.

'What is that?' asked a photographer, behind us. 'Where did that come from?'

'No idea,' I said. 'One of the catering staff must have let it slip off a tray.'

Molly, still being held, was doing cycling movements in the air, so eager was she to get to the treat. Matilda, forever a scavenger, was pulling on her lead to get to it first. Anna had both her hands full with Molly, so I reached over carefully, retrieved the meatball and popped it into Molly's open mouth. It had left a round impression in the wet cement.

Lifting up Matilda, I gently placed one of her fat, bulldog paws over the meatball impression so that it looked like a pad with surrounding claw marks. I then placed her other paw next to it. They didn't correspond and any future visitors to Harrods would wonder what ill-proportioned breed had been invited to commemorate the opening! We stood up, brushed down our dresses and the little group applauded.

'Come on,' I said. 'Let's go. The girls' paws will be here for perpetuity. Always having a hand in Harrods. That can't be bad.'

Coming out of Harrods to find George standing by the side of his battered Skoda, double-parked close to a Porsche, was pure delight. He looked so happy to be there and to be of service. He was dressed in a 50s-style pink salmon suit, and wearing the obligatory sunglasses, and was holding open the passenger door.

'Your carriage awaits,' he grinned. 'Where's Anna?'

'Heading home to pamper and prepare for the concert,' I said, letting Matilda on to the back seat. 'Right girls,' said George. 'I think supper in Soho, before work.'

Breaking every rule of the road by screeching into a U turn in the middle of Knightsbridge, and steering with only one hand, he pointed the Skoda towards the West End.

It was a weekday so the two of us had radio shows that night, and whereas I would have preferred to rest before heading into the BBC, George was, as usual, up for a party. His days had no schedule other than he had to be sitting behind the mic at 2 a.m.

The rest of his time was spent doing whatever he fancied, and being with me and Matilda was top of the list. Unfortunately, those opportunities were becoming fewer and fewer.

Behind the wheel, me by his side, Matilda on the back seat, her jowels resting on his shoulder, and the Rolling Stones playing loudly on the stereo, this was George at his happiest. In his mind, we were Bonnie and Clyde. All he needed to complete the fantasy was a pair of pistols strapped to Matilda.

'She smells of seaweed,' he said, patting her large head with one hand. 'What's she been up to?'

I looked over my shoulder and noticed a patch of dried sea-clay wrap on her ear.

'How was your medical?' I asked, changing the subject.

'Oh man, those posh doctors have you running everywhere. And it costs! Jeez, X-rays, then another consultation just to be told the results. Cost a bloody fortune. But I got a free latte.'

He lent forward and turned the stereo up a little.

'And?' I asked. 'What did they say?'

I couldn't understand why he was spinning it out like this, making me beg for details. I had absolutely no idea what he went to have checked, or why.

'I've broken my foot,' he said, 'probably by kicking a tree.'

'WHAT! What do you mean, you've broken your foot? You've been walking everywhere. And if it's broken, why the hell are you driving us in this car?'

'I've been limping, man,' he said. 'It's just you haven't been around long enough to notice. You're always out.'

I was dumbfounded. The foot was not set in plaster. Not even a bandage. He appeared to be in no obvious pain and he was wearing a celebratory pink suit. Was this just a ploy to get my attention?

'What tree did you kick?' I asked.

'The copper beech outside your flat,' George answered. 'Weeks ago.'

'Why?' I asked. 'Why did you kick it?'

'I'd locked myself out, remember?' he said. 'You were judging the Wet Nose Awards and I had to get the caretaker to let me in. It's only one of the small bones in my little toe. Nothing they can do about it.'

I was at a loss for words. This big old bloke had forked out for a private doctor to be told he had broken his little toe – the type of injury many people ignore and wait to mend. None of it made sense.

'George, why don't you register with a local doctor? Then you won't have to pay when you need a consultation.'

Without answering, he turned into Dean Street and pulled up right outside Bar Italia. One of the waiters, tray in hand, came scurrying up as George lent out of the window, and said, 'Ciao.'

It was obvious I'd touched a nerve and he wasn't going to give me a straight answer. His medical records were with his family doctor in Milton Keynes, and it looked as though that's where they would remain.

Sometimes George appeared to speak to me in riddles. He would give me snippets of information, but not all of it. I have no secrets. I believe myself to be an open book, often to my detriment. All aspects of my life were up for discussion, on and off air. The listeners knew almost as much about me as my family did. That's one of the features of late-night radio – it can often be accused of becoming confessional.

However, the more I got to know and love George, the more I realized there were parts of his life he would never reveal. Maybe, if I'd listened to his overnight show, I would have gleaned more information, but I was usually asleep. Occasionally, listeners would call in to my show and mention that he'd spoken about his son or his grandson and it would surprise me. Apparently, one day he'd talked about one of their excursions in London, but he'd never told me about this. Maybe his reluctance to mention his family in my presence was to save me from feeling compromised. He knew I never listened to his show.

His insistence that the family were accepting of his new life in London had convinced me that all was well. On the rare occasions when I asked him about his sons and their partners, he would go quiet. The heart attack, years earlier, and his wife consequently nursing him back to good health was all he was prepared to share.

Now I was becoming suspicious about just how severed his connections with his past life really were. Was he returning to the family doctor for regular check-ups? That would explain why he wouldn't register in London. Was his wife still acting as a confidante while, at the same time, he presented me with a clean bill of health? Maybe the story of a diagnosis of a broken toe in a private clinic was a cry for help, and for me to become more involved in his welfare. For 30 years he had been cosseted and cared for; now he had landed himself with an undomesticated, career-obsessed, dog enthusiast who was never at home. He seemed to thrive on my mad metropolitan lifestyle but my guess was that he was beginning to crave more attention.

Bar Italia excited him. It was easy to understand why. The place was pure theatre. We were given his usual table, outside, facing directly towards Ronnie Scott's. One by one the waiters came out to greet us and to fuss over Matilda. George had brought her here from a puppy and she loved all the adoration from the Soho crowd. The doorman from Ronnie Scott's always had dog biscuits in his pocket for the street dogs and he strutted over and offered one to Matilda.

'Mate, take a picture of us,' George said to him, wrapping his great arm around me and sitting Matilda on his lap.

This bar was George's office. When he wasn't at work or with me, he was here. He knew every detail of the place, the history of their 50-year-old Gaggia coffee machine and the name of each framed celebrity on the wall. I believe it was his secret desire to have his picture up there, beside the images of Leonardo diCaprio, Frankie Valli and Rocky Marciano. I know for a fact that he had given them a signed, framed photograph of himself, but they had still to find space for it on the overcrowded wall. In anyone else that would have been seen as an act of extreme arrogance, but with George it was simply down to his childlike awe of the place and his longing to be a part of it, forever.

Bar Italia never closed and often George would walk there straight from his show and enjoy a brandy with his breakfast. Occasionally, in the middle of my show, cabbies would come on air to say they had driven down Old Compton Street and spotted Big George and Matilda sitting outside the bar as part of their evening constitutional.

We had just ordered pizzas and a double brandy for George when my phone rang. I looked down and was surprised to see it was Y Bother.

'Hello,' I said.

'Where's Anna?' He sounded stressed.

'She went home to change and then to meet you,' I said, checking my watch and noticing it was nearly 8 p.m.

'I've been waiting outside the venue since seven and no sign of her. I called but her phone's turned off,' he said. 'I don't know what to do.'

'Hang on,' I said, and turning to George, 'Anna's not turned up,' trying not to sound panicked.

'Don't blame her. Neither would I for a Debbie Harry gig,' he said. 'Maybe she's had second thoughts.'

'She's been planning what to wear for weeks,' I said, then turning back to speak to Y Bother, 'Look, you go into the concert, I'll keep calling her. She's probably in a cab stuck in traffic.'

'I can't believe she wouldn't turn up,' he said, his voice rising. 'I really stuck my neck out for these tickets. I mean, this is the first time we've been out without Molly for a year. Christ, I can't believe I'm going to a Debbie Harry gig on my own!'

As he was talking, a text arrived.

'Look, I'll call you if I hear anything,' I said and hung up. The text was from Anna: MOLLY PASSING BLOOD CLOTS. FREAKING OUT. NOT GOING TO GIG.

The Fiorentina pizza placed in front of me held no appeal. I couldn't even pick up the cutlery. In Anna's world, this was the very worst thing that could ever happen. Molly's health, well-being and subsequent quality of life were Anna's motivation to survive. Nothing, not even her own welfare, was as important. I tried her number. It was on voicemail. I hung up. I knew what she'd done. In order to avoid the wrath of Y Bother, she'd turned her phone off.

George was ripping his pizza apart with his hands, stuffing slices into his mouth and feeding the crusts to Matilda. I ignored it. For once, I didn't care. Looking at my scavenging dog, I was simply thankful she appeared to be in good health. I couldn't imagine what Anna was going through. The mention of Molly's bladder problem earlier now made sense. But Anna's excitement about going out for the night had wiped it from my mind.

Since I'd known her, this was the first event without Molly that she had really looked forward to. It had come at the right time, or so I'd assumed. I thought it would be the olive branch to get Y Bother back in her favour and possibly back into her flat. That scenario was now drifting rapidly away. I tried her number again. This time she picked up.

'Anna, what's happened with Molly? Tell me,' I urged. Her answer came in a stream of indistinguishable sobs. I felt sick.

'Anna, I can't understand you,' I interrupted. 'Is Molly standing up or lying down?'

'I can't leave her, I can't,' Anna sobbed. 'Nobody understands.'

'Right, I'm coming over,' I said. 'I'll get George to drive me. When you hear me knock, let me in.'

I hung up before she had a chance to object and turned to face George. He was raising a glass of brandy to a passing transsexual on the way to Madame Jo Jo's. His plate was empty and Matilda looked replete.

'George, you have to drive me to Anna's,' I said, grabbing Matilda's lead.

'What? Oh man, must I?' he said. 'We've got the best table and anyway, you've got a show to do in a couple of hours. Tell her to feed Molly chicken or take her to the emergency vet.'

I knew that when it came to Molly, I couldn't tell Anna to do anything. It was where she drew the line. I bowed to her greater knowledge as far as the health of either of our dogs was concerned. I also knew that if I waited for a cab, I would be really stuck for time, and I had to be at work by 10 p.m.

'Come on, George. Drop me off, then you can come back here with Matilda.'

Grudgingly he threw some money on the table and walked across to the parked Skoda. I noticed he still wasn't limping.

'Man, this is crazy,' said George as we headed down Upper Street. 'Anna has got to stay cool. Molly's middle-aged, she's going to get ill. Dogs get sick. Are you going to go racing off every time she's under the weather?'

In my head I was shouting, 'SHUT UP! SHUT UP!'

George would never get his head around it. This was Anna and Molly. There was no comparison. They were joined by an umbilical cord. Nobody, not me or Y Bother or even her family, meant as much to Anna as Molly did.

When she opened the front door, she was still wearing her new cerise matching boots and jeans. Three Carmen curlers with pins were stuck, haphazardly, in her hair and her face was white with stress. She turned back into the flat and left me to follow her down the corridor to the living room.

In the corner, near the radiator, Molly was lying, panting slightly, on her leopard-skin daybed. Instead of bounding towards me as usual, she lifted her head and looked guiltily into my eyes. It was a look of 'Sorry, this has mucked things up for everyone, hasn't it?'

Anna knelt down by the bed and started to rub Molly under the chin. I stood looking down at them.

'I took her out for a final pee before I called a cab,' she said. 'And two massive clots of blood appeared, separate from the urine. I knew she was feeling under the weather because she wouldn't eat her dinner. This has been on the cards for some time.'

Looking around me, I could see the abandoned preparations Anna had made for Molly's 'home alone' evening – rubber Kong toys stuffed with the inevitable meatball treats, calves hooves scattered across the carpet – but also what looked like a row of small, medicinal-type phials.

Realistically, I was buying myself time before asking for any more details. Past experience had shown me that where Molly's health was concerned, I should never offer advice or appear to know more that Anna. Her happy disposition changed when her dog's wellbeing was compromised, and she turned into a human hand grenade. I took a deep breath.

'Have you called the vet?' I asked tentatively.

Anna removed her hand from Molly's head and looked up at me. She was ashen.

'I'm taking her in for an X-ray first thing tomorrow morning.' She stood up and fetched one of the phials. 'I've got homeopathic remedies and Rupert's on the way. He's going to perform some immediate acupuncture. It will help balance her and he can test her levels.'

Rupert was a regular guest on our show, offering advice to listeners on alternative medicine. He had been a practising vet before moving across to acupuncture and holistic medicine. Such was his popularity and success that he took appointments on a referral basis only.

I knew Anna used him as a counsellor and confidant regarding Molly, and the respect they had for each other was evident. She trusted his opinions because he had a background of traditional as well as alternative medicine, and he saw in her a well-informed, intelligent owner, who was not going to be brainwashed by science.

'He has recommended I give her one Cantharsis every ten minutes for the first hour. Then it's one every thirty minutes for the next four hours,' she said, tipping Molly's head back and popping one in. 'Rupert and I have been trying to diagnose this for some time,' she told me. 'I wanted to avoid taking her to the vet because of her fear of them, and also because I prefer to try alternative. I didn't want to worry you, especially when we have such a busy diary.'

Trying to absorb all the details, I marvelled at the way Molly obligingly swallowed her pills. No wonder Anna had cancelled the gig. The hourly regime was going to prevent her from sleeping, let alone leaving the house.

I was confused to know how to play this. Part of me wanted to adopt George's take on the situation and tell her to get a grip. But if I wanted our friendship to continue, I knew that wasn't the way. I also knew nothing I could say or do would help. I could only listen and be there while she carried on with the plans she had made for Molly's recovery. Her phone started to ring.

'That will be Y Bother. I can't talk to him,' she said, her voice rising into panic.

'You need to tell him you're okay,' I said. 'He's worried and at a gig that was meant for you.'

'I can't, I can't,' she cried. 'He doesn't understand. Molly has to have me here. There's no way I can leave her while she's like this.'

Her phone stopped. Then mine started.

'He's calling me,' I said, checking the phone. 'Anna, I must speak to him. He deserves to know what's happened.'

She turned her back on me and knelt down with Molly. I couldn't possibly speak to him within earshot of Anna, so I pushed open the patio doors, went out and stood under the washing line to answer his call. I could hardly hear him against the background noise of crowd and dodgy music.

'It's me,' he shouted. 'What's happened? Are you with her?'

'Molly's ill,' I shouted back. 'She can't be left. I'm with them both now.'

For a moment, all I could hear were the distant sounds of Debbie Harry singing an unrecognizable song. She must have been trying out new material. When Y Bother spoke again, his voice was much quieter. I could barely hear him.

'I knew it. I knew it would be Molly.' He sounded resigned. 'Is she going to be okay?'

I assumed he meant Anna.

'The acupuncturist is on the way,' I said. 'I'll stay until he gets here.'

'Acupuncturist?' he shouted. 'What acupuncturist? When did she start seeing an acupuncturist?'

I assumed he meant Molly.

'A guy called Rupert. Actually, he's very nice. I'd trust him,' I said.

A pause, and another unrecognizable lyric.

'Jo, I tried, I really tried,' Y Bother said. 'I thought this evening everything would be back to normal. That we would have a blast. It was all for her. I don't even like Debbie Harry.'

At that moment Anna walked out on to the patio and lit a cigarette. I motioned for her to come and have a word with Y Bother.

'It's the least he deserves,' I hissed. 'He's waiting for you. Just speak to him.'

She recoiled like a terrified cat.

'Here's Anna,' I said abruptly. 'Just to have a quick word with you.' I shoved my phone into her hand. She stood rigid, took a deep breath then launched in.

'I'm not coming to the gig,' she shouted. 'Molly's passing haematoma clots from her "frou frou".' Anna's voice was building to a crescendo. 'I'll kill myself if you make me go to the gig. In fact, I'll kill myself when Molly dies, which won't be long now – and it's all my fault! So get used to me not being around. Sorry.'

She slapped the phone into my hand and ran back indoors. That was an Anna I hardly recognized. If I didn't know she meant every word of it, I'd have laughed at the melodrama. No wonder Y Bother had moved out.

I put the phone back to my ear and I could hear Y Bother's panicked breath, even over the musical din. I felt quite sorry for him.

'Go and enjoy the free hospitality,' I said. 'And blag her a T-shirt.'

Then I hung up.

In an hour I was expected to be in the studio to prepare for my show and I had no means of transport. I would have to find a cab. The activities of the day, and now the worry of Molly, were beginning to take effect and the four hours of broadcasting still to come were exhausting to think about. But I knew Anna couldn't be left in her present state and I needed to stay until Rupert, the Messiah, arrived.

Molly seemed to have perked up a little and was resting her chin on the arm of the sofa while Anna was concentrating hard on shaking out another homeopathic pill. Under her breath she seemed to be reciting some sort of mantra. 'One every ten minutes for sixty minutes, one every ten minutes for sixty minutes,' she repeated, rattling the phial.

'Oh Lord,' I thought, 'she's flipped.' I waited for her to tip the little white pill down Molly's obliging throat.

'Anna,' I said. 'Molly isn't going to die. Believe me. You really have to pull yourself together. For her sake as well as yours.'

It sounded like a script straight from *Holby City*. Why, in moments of high drama, does everything sound clichéd?

She put down the little glass phial and began patting Molly's long noble neck. I held my breath.

'I have tried to explain to Y Bother that Molly is all I need. He doesn't understand that she takes up all my emotional energy. I don't have room for anyone else. She is now ten and not as hearty, and this bladder thing is a major concern. I need to give her all my attention.'

She was rubbing Molly's neck so hard during this speech that surplus fur descended to the carpet and collected in a small pile.

'But Anna, that's not normal,' I burst out, realizing, with surprise, that I appeared now to be siding with Y Bother. 'You're still young and groovy and you should be having loads of sex and sharing your life. It's not good for you to live on your own with just Molly.'

I felt her anger before I heard it. She stood up and turned what can only be described as 'red eye' on me.

'And you would know would you?' she said with control. 'Have you looked at your relationship recently? It seems to me that George is just an extra worry.' She was almost spitting the words out. How long, I wondered, had she been storing this up? 'Wouldn't you find life a whole lot easier if it was just you and Matilda?' she continued. 'Without constantly having to take his calls or tell him where you are?'

Ding! Ding! Right on cue a text arrived, inevitably from George. I had to brace myself to look. It was a photograph of a dish of Italian ice cream and the words, 'my pudding'.

'Yes,' I said quietly, deleting the text. 'Sometimes I feel we're going to explode, the three of us living in such a tiny space. But he's fantastic with Matilda, and there have been times when I couldn't have done the job I do if he wasn't there to look after her.'

DING! DING! Another text. This time a photo of some left over panetone on the table: THE CRUMBS YOU THROW AT ME WHEN YOU FEEL LIKE IT. Oh no, was he drunk, maudlin or both? What was this about? He'd seemed fine when he dropped me off.

Anna slumped back down on to the sofa. One of her remaining curlers plopped out. Molly jumped up next to her and wrapped herself into a ball with her long nose tucked under her paws.

'Y Bother loves Molly, I know he does,' she said. 'But there is such jealousy between them. And I'm afraid if I have to choose, it will always be Molly, and he can't tolerate that. Last week he turned up here, drunk, and tipped all of her homeopathic remedies down the loo.'

I tried not to laugh. She seemed calmer and it was time I left. I'd have to call George to come and collect me because I realized

I didn't have enough cash for a cab. One storm beginning to calm and I sensed another on the horizon.

I'd just gone into the hall to make the call when Anna's front door opened and in walked Rupert, flustered and, I was quick to notice, without knocking. I'd forgotten how young and fresh-faced he was compared to our usual cronies. He hugged me at precisely the same time as George answered my call, so he went in to greet Anna and Molly.

'George,' I said apprehensively. 'Do you mind coming to collect me? I'm still at Anna's and I need to be at work in thirty minutes and I haven't got enough on me for a cab.'

He didn't answer. I could hear talking and music in the background.

'George?' I repeated. 'Are you there?'

'Look,' he said, and I knew, immediately, he was not sober. 'I've turned into a mug. Man, I tried to send you a picture of one but Mario says they only have espresso cups.'

There was a thump, as though an arm had landed on a table.

'You're breaking my heart, man. Do you understand, breaking my heart? I can't keep being picked up and put down.'

Ironically, he must have put his phone down. It went dead. I was stranded. Speechless, I turned round to share my dilemma with Anna. She and Rupert and Molly were all on the sofa, happy.

CHAPTER 5

'They'll think we're lesbians.'

George moved out in the same month as Crufts. It was a time of mixed emotions. Days filled with dogs and despair.

Barking at the Moon had the honour of being the first radio show to broadcast live from the event, in the Birmingham NEC. All the planning and pestering had finally paid off. Our radio show, along with the Sky television series, was gradually carving us a reputation. Maybe George sensed the warning signs that my life was going to become even more hectic, forcing our relationship into more compromises. Who knows?

He obviously didn't want his nose rubbed in it, and not long after the night of the Debbie Harry concert, I returned home from filming to find his suits, guitars and bottles of brandy all gone. The place looked how I'd always wanted it to look – neat. But it also looked boring and dull.

Matilda, as usual, had raced expectantly ahead and come to an abrupt halt. She stood, taking in the lack of mess, and looked up at me.

'No idea,' I murmured to her, then moved over to the bed. On the pillow was a photograph taken in New York's Union Square of George and me, laughing together. I turned it over, knowing he would have written something in his customary felt tip: YOU NEED SPACE. MOVING INTO A PAD IN A COUPLE OF DAYS. TIL THEN, SLEEPING IN CAR. I LOVE YOU.

This was typical George. Dramatic. Who, in his 50s, working for the BBC, sleeps in his car? Did he see himself as Marylebone's Outlaw Josie Wales? Besides, his Residents Parking allowed him to park in a certain zone of Westminster that was well lit. He'd be asleep in full view of everyone.

Having yearned for a quiet flat to come home to, I now grabbed Matilda and walked back out. I felt anxious. George had been getting under my feet but he was my favourite person to be with and, apart from the lack of space, he was a laugh to have around. And, of course, I loved him and I didn't want him living far away.

His new home was at the other end of my street. From my roof terrace I could see his building – a mansion block of similar architecture to mine. I'm on the third floor but his new flat was in the basement. He looked out at the feet of passers-by making their way towards Bloomsbury.

As far as space was concerned, it was a tiny bit bigger than mine, with a bed that pulled down from the wall and 70s furniture, belonging to the landlord. Cheap paintings of landscapes, and dried flowers in the fireplace, gave it a feeling of 'rented accommodation', but that didn't bother George. Interior design was never a concern for him.

The block employed a live-in caretaker, ex-army. Ian was middle-aged and lived in the flat next door to George's. He was a local character and I'd spotted him previously around the neighbourhood. George admired Ian's military-style running of the block, especially the way he Brassoed every railing and handle each morning early, before breakfast.

'Ian's a top geezer,' George assured me. 'He's shown me where he hides his Brasso and his bin bags under the stairs and says I can help myself whenever I want.'

Such generosity, along with their mutual love of brandy, led the two of them to become unlikely but respectful friends.

I was intrigued that the monitor to the building's CCTV was on Ian's bedside table. When he wasn't emptying bins or rubbing Brasso on railings, he was able to monitor every visitor.

It took George four minutes to walk from his front door to mine; slightly longer if he was with Matilda. Just time enough for me to apply lipstick.

His decision to move out came as no surprise. He would have said, if asked, that I'd been pushing him further and further away by my absence and therefore giving him fewer days with Matilda. In my mind, it was all down to workload. If I could have spent more time with George, I would have done, but our timetables were crazy. George did his four hours on the overnight show, while I slept. When he got back, I was usually up and out. After sleeping, the rest of his day was left for leisure. Occasionally, he would meet with musician mates for a jam session in the guitar shop in Denmark Street or to discuss musician union matters, but usually he would hang about, hoping to spend time with me.

My days, on the other hand, due to the Sky series, were spent filming with Anna and Molly. At weekends we were often opening dog shows or working on a running order for Thursday's *Barking at the Moon*. Amid all this, I also had to prepare and present my own four-hour late-night radio show. On Saturdays I presented a breakfast show. I was too scared to turn down work, and besides, I was loving all of it.

Unfortunately, the only time left to see George was when he acted as a chauffeur. He would always be there if I needed collecting or dropping off and didn't have my car. I was fully aware that this was exploiting his good nature, but at the same time, I patronizingly thought he enjoyed feeling useful.

Initially, this was the case, but over the months he had observed Y Bother's relationship with Anna and much of it resonated with him. The night of the Debbie Harry concert was a turning point and had convinced him that he would never be so publicly duped. So, to maintain some sense of dignity, he had decided to find a place of his own, somewhere close by. Secretly, I was relieved.

'This could be quite sexy,' I told him. 'We have to make an appointment to see each other.'

'So, what's new?' he'd answered.

However big a jolt this was for him and however much he would have preferred to be under my roof, I knew he was excited to have a place of his own. Living alone was a novelty for him. I'd spent most of my life living solo, but for George, this was a whole new experience. Until the age of 18 he had shared a room with his brother and when he moved out it was to get married.

'My fridge will always be stacked with champagne and ice lollies for visitors, man, and I'm never drawing the curtains,' he said with childish delight.

He was a bloke true to his word. While my flat was girlie and light, his became a sort of playpen-styled bunker. The musty curtains remained closed so no daylight filtered through, and the flat was lit by a single, overhead bulb. I often tripped when I walked in because every bit of floor space was covered in musical instruments, sound equipment and electrical leads.

One of my favourite bras (chewed by Matilda) dangled from a banjo, which itself hung on the redundant fireplace. My embarrassment at seeing it there was curbed by his insistence that it helped him to know I'd once worn it. So the bra remained as a kind of art installation.

Not for the first time, I thought of his wife. Had she employed a cleaner? Had he always lived in such turmoil? Had she followed him around picking up pants? Something I would never do.

His pull-down bed was left pulled down and, surprisingly for me, laid with pristine Egyptian cotton sheets. This had been my only proviso. I'd insisted that if he wanted me to stay the night, I needed to know that at least the linen was spotless.

Underneath the bed, however, existed an alien world that became Matilda's den. She would spend hours under there, dragging various objects with her and sniffing his random socks. Once, reaching underneath while trying to retrieve an earring, I found an uneaten hard-boiled egg.

Matilda loved staying at George's and would either curl up on his 1970's scruffy sofa or dive straight into her den. He couldn't care less where she left dog hair or footprints. She was liberated. His gaffe was where the fun was. In mine, there were too many rules.

'I'm putting the kettle on,' he would bellow at me down the phone. 'Come and have a quick cuppa and I'll walk you back.'

In a way, we were courting all over again. Matilda and I would set off down the street, leaving George four minutes to kick everything under the bed in preparation. Then, as we approached the block, she would bound up the steps to his block's front door in time to hear him shout, 'Hurrah,' through the entry phone. I always loved the fact he would be listening out to hear our footsteps on the pavement in time to shout the hurrah.

Occasionally, we would arrive to the welcoming scent of a Jo Malone grapefruit candle that had been placed randomly in the midst of all the chaos. Gestures such as this he made to please me – a bottle of pomegranate handwash balanced strategically on a sink full of shaving scum alongside an incongruous pink hand towel. They stood out in their clumsiness but so did he and I loved him for it.

Initially, our relationship improved. When I went back to work after a quick pop down to his for a cuppa, I would often leave Matilda behind so that he could later walk her back up to my flat. Somehow, having Matilda to himself, in a place of his own, meant our time apart didn't depress him quite so much. He would still text and call throughout the day but he was no longer surrounded by my possessions and confronted by my absence. There was no more kicking of trees.

'If you've got two nights booked in a Brum hotel, I might take the time off and stay up there with you,' George said as the day of Crufts approached. 'I could swim and use the facilities while you're sticking rosettes on mutts and then we can groove in the evening. There's a bangin' club in the Bull Ring. I once jammed there with Mott the Hoople.'

I stared at him as though he had just landed from Mars. The two days at Crufts were so manic that we had organized them like a military manoeuvre. Every hour was accounted for, with interviews, pre-records, judging and a live radio show. Our

Crufts *Barking at the Moon* broadcast was to be a full four hours. A romantic two-day break followed by head banging in a Brummie dive was not on the agenda.

'We have adjoining rooms in the Holiday Inn on site,' Anna had told me the previous night. 'They make it dog friendly throughout the event. Many of the competitors will be staying there.'

She was in her stride now. This was the highlight of Anna's professional and personal calendar. I listened, impressed, as she took control.

'I'm going up the night before because I'm planning to arrive at the arena on the first day very early,' she continued. 'I have a new client with a range of doggy toothbrushes who needs my help. I may have to assist by demonstrating the circular action on Molly. She has the teeth of a two year old so there's no better model. We've got Access All Areas for the girls, so please remember to hang Matilda's pass around her neck. Call me the moment you arrive!'

This was to be my first Crufts – over 22,000 dogs representing approximately 200 Kennel Club registered breeds, making it the biggest dog show in the world. I had no idea what to expect. Filling half of the NEC, Crufts is the second biggest exhibition in the UK, and over 160,000 people visit every year. It was incredible to think there had never been a radio show broadcasting from there.

Both the Kennel Club and the BBC had agreed to our live radio broadcast. In true local-radio style, no extra money was available for an outside broadcast, so it was down to Anna and me to make it happen. We didn't want to push our luck or rock the boat by making demands. The BBC had already withdrawn from transmitting the show on television.

Mel, our loyal producer, was going to travel up on the day of the broadcast. There would be a phone operator back at base and an engineer to drive the show, but no researchers and no other on-site technical help. The Kennel Club had offered us their own sound engineers but, legally, they weren't allowed to operate BBC equipment. We were on our own.

Had it been a daytime show, there would have been no problems, but *Barking at the Moon* went out at 10 p.m. and the venue closed at 7 p.m. Therefore, our main concern was filling the first two hours of a four-hour live show with guests and expecting them to stay behind until midnight after a hectic day in the main halls. Ideally, on the running order, we wanted a couple of winning competitors and then colourful people with good life stories. The final two hours would be the usual phone-in with just callers.

My journey to Crufts didn't start well. Matilda and I managed to get lost in early morning rush-hour traffic on Spaghetti Junction, and overshot the turning to the Birmingham NEC. I called Anna. She was on voicemail, obviously preoccupied with demonstrating how to remove tartar from the teeth of a beagle.

I needed to get back on to the M6 but was confused by the city centre signs, which all seemed to be pointing back the way I'd come. A Volvo estate pulled into the centre lane in front of me and

I noticed a sticker reading DALMATIANS IN TRANSIT on the back window. Underneath it, three pairs of quizzical eyes peered out. They had to be competitors, I decided, so I followed the dalmatians and, sure enough, we travelled a few miles further and then they turned off towards a massive sign saying NEC, with me tucked in behind them. My phone rang. It was Anna.

'Where are you?' She sounded very excited over all the crowd noise.

'Sorry,' I said. 'I managed to get lost coming into the city but I'm back on course now. I should be at the hotel in a few minutes. I'll drop off my stuff and make my way to the exhibition centre.'

'Coolio,' she said. 'I'll come over to the hotel and meet you. I've already fixed us a guest for tonight. A Marilyn Monroe lookalike with a toy poodle called JFK.'

'I know them,' I said, about to hang up, 'They are a drag act from Brighton.'

'Wait,' shouted Anna. 'I've got some major good news. Tell you when I see you. Whoop!'

This was Anna's war cry of joy. She used it when something nice happened or if Molly had mastered another physical feat. I was beginning to get quite excited myself. The cars in front and to the side of mine were mostly full of dogs or covered in canine branding. We were all heading into the same car park.

For most of the year this mediocre hotel is a stopping place for commercial travellers and businessmen, but for the next four days it would be dedicated to the dog world. Walking into reception I was greeted by two giant Afghan hounds seated at the desk, both with curlers in their hair. Waiting with its owner by the front door, for a taxi, was a Pyrenean mountain dog wearing paper leggings and a cape. Oh joy! It seemed the lunatics really had taken over the asylum. This was my kind of hotel. Lingering smells of breakfast from the dining room mingled with those of damp dog but more evident than the odour was a real sense of purpose from breeders and handlers, all preparing to head off to the main arena.

Anna and Molly were there to greet us, both wearing their Access All Areas passes and big grins on their faces. Matilda bounded over and Anna and I hugged as though this was about to be the most exciting adventure of our lives. I checked in and we all headed towards the lifts.

'Do you want the good news or the brilliant news?' asked Anna. 'First,' she went on, not waiting for me to reply, 'the Kennel Club has given us the whole of the press suite to broadcast from tonight. The rest of the place will be locked up. They have also laid on three security guys to guide the guests into and out of the car park.'

I nodded, thinking that by 10 p.m. when the place was closed, we were going to have to create some semblance of atmosphere. Molly couldn't keep her barking up for four hours. Maybe I should have packed the BBC tape of back ground noises.

'But the big surprise for us is Balding is on board! Whoop!' She started to jump up and down.

I was still none the wiser.

'Clare Balding has agreed to do an interview with us on her Channel 4 show!' Anna was now hopping joyously on one leg. This, to her, was like getting an audience with the Pope.

'Whoop!' she cried again. 'Her producer said they will schedule it for tomorrow.'

This was very good news. Clare Balding's show was going out daily on Channel 4, live from the event, and attracted a good few million viewers around the world. Getting our faces on her show would give us some much-needed credibility in the dog world.

The lift doors opened and there, confronting us, were two Siberian huskies. Nothing takes your breath away quite as much as sharing a lift with a pair of beautiful, wolf-like creatures while keeping your own bull breeds under control. Their piercing blue eyes watched our every move as the four people, four dogs and luggage squeezed into the small space. We got out at level 2 and Molly couldn't resist murmuring one of her low grumble growls – which basically said, 'You might look like a wolf, but don't forget I'm a bull terrier.'

We dumped my bags in the hotel room. Both Molly and Matilda had picked up on our excitement and began jumping on and off the bed and then, as Anna opened her adjoining door, they ran between the two rooms barking and chasing each other. As ever, there was a strong smell of green tripe permeating from Anna's room.

Spread out on her dressing table I couldn't help but notice Molly's various homeopathic remedies. These had increased since the bladder complaint, but looking at her now, turning circles and chasing her own tail, she was obviously not suffering. I didn't comment. If Molly was on form, then Anna was happy.

My phone started and before answering it, I knew it would be George.

'I've just found a dead mouse under my bed,' he said. 'By the look of it, it's been there for a few days.'

'Oh George, you must employ a cleaner. It's not good living among dead rodents,' I said, wrinkling my nose.

'Nah, I'm not poncing about with cleaners,' he replied. 'How's it going? What's the hotel like?'

'Doggy,' I answered. 'George, it really isn't worth your while coming up here. Anna and I are going to be racing around the show like maniacs.'

'I could keep an eye on Matilda for you,' he said. 'I'm getting cabin fever stuck in this apartment.'

My heart sank. I'd thought that with a place of his own, these couple of days away would be easier for him to deal with. Obviously, I was wrong.

'Try and listen to our show tonight,' I said. 'Let me know how it sounds. We may be the first-ever radio show to broadcast live from Crufts, but it'll be from an empty press suite. I'm worried it'll sound dead. I'll have my phone on, so text me if we sound rubbish.'

But he had gone. Whether it was Paris or Birmingham, a night without him in a hotel filled me with guilt and him with loneliness.

'What was that about?' asked Anna.

'He wants to come up here for a dirty weekend,' I answered.

'What?' exclaimed Anna. 'There's no time for sex! We've so much to get through. Get Fit with Fido is tomorrow night and that's when we appear with Balding on Channel 4.'

So keep fit with George was to be replaced with Get Fit with Fido, and to be honest, I couldn't have been more relieved. These days I looked forward to my bed just to collapse in and sleep.

Crufts was everything I wanted it to be. My workplace for half my life has been radio or television studios. I actually feel at home in them. I had never set foot in an exhibition centre let alone worked in one. I'd never been to Earls Court to visit Ideal Home exhibitions or food fayres. This was all new to me.

I'd introduced Anna to my world; now she was showing me hers. Right from the time when, as a teenager, she had accompanied her dad on RSPCA business, and through all her adult life, she had hung about show rings. A groovy rock chick on the outside, she travelled between London and Paris, and very few of her mates knew that her weekends were mainly spent competing at dog shows. Keeping herself to herself, usually on her own, this had been her 'other' life. Watching her now, shouting over the racket from tinny Tannoys among the doggy mayhem, I could see that she looked totally at home.

Our attire was completely out of sorts. Always with an eye on our image, we were decked out in Diane Von Furstenberg wrap-around dresses and heels. Among the fleeces, flat shoes and short haircuts, we looked quite incongruous, but any floating fans managed to spot us immediately.

Anna took the lead, striding forward with Molly and flaunting the laminated passes. It was only as we'd approached the entrance that I'd realized how clever she had been to acquire Access All Areas, not just for us, but also for the dogs. At this event, not even the competing or show dogs may cross the shiny piazza area of the NEC, but ours had been given special dispensation, having been catagorized as BBC radio co-hosts. It meant the passes had to be scrutinized every time we went through, and secretly, we took great pleasure in showing our bright AAA laminates – it left the security guards scratching their heads as they allowed us to march, inappropriately, on stilettos, through the barriers. Eventually, of course, being stopped each time drove us to distraction!

It was only 9 a.m. but the competitors, along with the public, were already flooding in through the doors. The noise was overpowering.

Surrounding the main show rings, hundreds of stalls were set up, selling dog-related merchandise from grooming tools to portraiture. Absolutely anything you might need for your pooch was available. The inventiveness of canine entrepeneurs was on show everywhere, from Anna's client's finger-puppet-styled toothbrush to a post-portal air freshener designed to hang from your dog's tail. Many of the companies had commissioned Anna to handle their PR when they were starting off, and as we made our way through the crowds, stallholders would stop her for a chat and to make a fuss of Molly. I was fascinated to see the respect she was being given by those on this commercial side of the dog world. Her insistence that she would never promote anything she wouldn't use on her own dog had often amused me, with all the gadgets we were expected to trial, but for her reputation, it had obviously paid off. The popularity of the stalls was proof enough that in a double-dip recession, the dog market really is one that flourishes.

We had until 6 p.m. to find contributors for our broadcast that night. These people would have to be prepared to stay behind in an empty exhibition centre until the early hours of the morning. At 7 p.m., when our producer, Mel, was due to arrive, we would set up our kit in the press office, type up the running order and scripts and prepare for the show.

Anna had suggested the benches would be the best place to recruit. This is where the dog handlers 'camp' for the day, surrounded by all the paraphernalia needed to prepare their dogs before entering the show ring.

A beautiful Irish setter, Bonnie, who had won her class, sat beside her proud owner, Bob, from Harrogate. Bob set aside his packed lunch to chat to us about his winning moment. Anna took her time before asking, 'Bob, would you be able to join us on air, in the press office, to talk about your experience in the ring?'

Bob paused, weighing the two of us up.

'I don't see why not,' he said. 'What time would you like me?'

'About one-ish,' I answered, knowing it couldn't be this easy.

'I'll go to the little boys room, have a coffee and I'll be right over.' He started to pack up his Tupperware.

'Oh no, Bob,' said Anna. 'That's one in the morning, not this afternoon.'

Bob's expression really said it all.

'I've had a thought,' said Anna, as we patrolled the rest of the benches. 'I can always ask Rupert to come on air and talk about acupuncture.'

'Is he up here?' I asked. This was the first mention of him at Crufts. 'Rupert to the Rescue' was how I was beginning to see him – always around in a crisis.

'Not yet, but I'm sure he will be dropping by at some point,' she answered. 'He usually does demonstrations with the Blue Cross.'

Well, at least that meant we had someone to fall back on. Rupert could be our plan B.

Filling the show was never going to be easy. Everybody wants their 15 minutes of fame, but only in daylight; not, it appeared, in the early hours of the morning. Confidently believing that you speculate to accumulate, we began handing out our business cards, announcing the time and place of the broadcast, encouraging anyone who had a story to tell, or a product to promote, to turn up.

By lunchtime, Anna's rent boy was still the only 'definite'. And if between then and midnight he struck lucky, we wouldn't even have him.

We had wandered out to the dog-run area so the dogs could pee. Since the onset of Molly's bladder problem, Anna scrutinized every one of her dog's pees for signs of blood. I held my breath, watching the stress in Anna's shoulders, and prayed that today would be a blood-free day.

For our whole time at Crufts, thank heavens, it was. On the days when blood was present, I knew Anna would be totally distracted. The homeopathic remedies appeared to be controlling it, but required Anna to encourage Molly to swallow clusters of little white pills every hour. I had learned to keep quiet. Somehow, she and the much-adored Rupert were keeping 10-year-old Molly's health on track.

Leaning against a wall, puffing on a fag and watching a pair of huskies sniffing about, was a tanned, fit-looking young bloke.

'Got a spare fag?' Anna asked him. 'Are those two yours?' she added, looking at the handsome dogs.

He nodded and offered her a Marlborough. I left them to it and concentrated on Matilda. Hopefully, Anna would work her charm and entice husky man to join us on the show. We were now all but soliciting on behalf of the BBC. Minutes later she called me over to join them.

'Jo, this is Heinrich. He's part of the husky display team. They're demonstrating a new aerodynamic sleigh in ten minutes.'

We shook hands. He was indeed very handsome.

'Heinrich has asked if I would help him out with the display,' said Anna. 'I said that's cool but only if he and his mate agree to come on tonight's show.'

I burst out laughing. Help him out? I bet she would!

'Anna, what do you know about sleighs?' I mocked. 'Are you going to ride on one with a whip and wearing thigh boots?'

Heinrich grinned, stubbing out his fag. We followed him to one of the smaller rings where 'The Husky Display with Sleigh' was to take place. Anna's role, according to Heinrich, was simply to run by the side of the sleigh, waving to the crowd. She would be a blonde outrider, a bit of eye candy among the dogs and the testosterone.

'If I was in the crowd, I'd be far more interested in the beautiful huskies than an ageing blonde,' confessed Anna, as she gathered with the team by the entrance to the ring. 'Thank heavens I'm not pulling, just waving.'

From the looks Heinrich and his mate were giving her, I reckoned she still had pulling power.

A crowd of three or four hundred husky enthusiasts had seated themselves around the ring in anticipation of the display. One of the attractions of Crufts is that there is a constant choice of events running throughout the day. Spectators drift from one ringside to another, and the growing appeal of huskies had drawn quite a lot of interest to this particular display.

Keeping hold of Molly and Matilda, I crept in behind two hefty girls in the second row, so as not to be seen and therefore distract Anna. Guilt was beginning to creep in when I thought of how much preparation for the broadcast we should have been doing. But if Heinrich kept his promise, we'd be okay, and nothing was going to prevent me from watching Anna Webb and a husky display team.

Somebody blew on the mic and strains of *Hall of the Mountain King* burst forth over the scratchy Tannoy. Struggling to be heard above it, an elderly commentator was also competing against the sound bleeding in from other loudspeakers dotted around the hall. In the end, he gave up and let the music do its job.

We in the crowd cheered as a flimsy curtain was drawn back to reveal the two huskies we had seen earlier, harnessed to a chariot-type sleigh. Heinrich, wearing snow goggles, was seated in the chariot, holding the reins, waiting to drive the impressive dogs. As the music surged so they began their lap of honour and thus Anna was revealed, also wearing snow goggles, running and waving beside the dogs.

'Woof! Woof!' she shouted to the crowd. A few 'Woof! Woofed!' back. Not many.

'Is she for real?' one of the hefty girls asked her friend.

There followed a very impressive Siberian display. At the end, the chariot came to a halt, Heinrich raised his ornamental whip and the huskies obediently lay down. We, the spectators, showed our appreciation, bursting into spontaneous applause. I remember Anna once telling me how huskies are one of the most difficult breeds to train. Even behind her goggles I could see how impressed she was with their 'lie down'.

The display team now posed in a frozen tableau, apart from Anna who, obviously getting into the mood, did a little Russian-style kick and flick of the hand. Heinrich yelled, 'Giddup,' and the huskies stood to attention. The now deafening strains of *Hall of the Mountain King* burst from the Tannoy, and chariot, dogs and Anna set off for a final encore lap. We applauded even louder and both hefty girls put their fingers in their mouths and whistled.

Molly, by my side, who loved clapping, started her celebratory barking. Matilda was asleep and snoring under my seat but Molly was throwing herself into the moment with abandon, causing those sitting next to me to snigger. However, Anna's antennae were on alert. The moment she heard Molly she looked over in our direction. I waved, hoping it would keep her calm. I have had full custody of Anna's dog only a handful of times and this was one of them. I knew Molly was fine and really enjoying herself, but for

Anna, any sign that her dog is distressed or likely to bolt and alarm bells start ringing. In other words, she was ready to freak out.

In my own feeble way, I attempted to quieten Molly.

'Good girl, Molls, now let's be quiet, good girl.'

Molly thought my talking to her was even more fun, and her barks were becoming even more excited.

The huskies and chariot were now on the move. The whole ensemble was heading round the ring at one hell of a pace. The noise of applause, cheering and Molly's barking was reaching a crescendo, but I could see that all Anna had on her mind was to get to where we were and calm her dog. Neither of us are certain if it was the goggles, her high heels or the sash of the Diane Von Furstenberg dress, but the next thing I see is her tumbling right over a husky. With a soft thud she landed face down in the sand, her dress flying up over her head. An audible 'Oh' came from the crowd.

'Serves her right,' said one of the hefties in front of me. 'She's a right show-off.'

Heinrich halted the huskies and took off his goggles in order to see better.

Watching my friend brush herself down, all I could think at the time was what amazingly white knickers she had on, so she had nothing to be ashamed of. Anna, however, was mortified.

'Let's hope nobody from the Kennel Club saw that,' she hissed as we made our way back to the press office, 'or we could jeopardize our status.'

What was certain was that if we didn't soon draw up a list of contributors for that night's broadcast, we wouldn't have a status with either the Kennel Club or the BBC. I wasn't sure if we could rely on Heinrich and his mates showing up following *that* performance.

All in all, we had handed out over 50 of our business cards to breeders, competitors and stallholders, with an invitation to join us from 10 p.m. in the makeshift radio studio. Many had pleaded exhaustion after the first full-on day of the event, but a few had agreed to consider it. All we could do was wait and see. We checked that our ISDN lines were compatible and ran through a few details with the engineer back at base, who would be driving the show.

The afternoon was drawing to an end and we were beginning to flag. The noise and crowds combined with the miles of walking through the halls to toilet break the dogs had taken their toll, but we had to stay at the show, instead of popping back to the hotel for a break, to wait for Mel, our producer. Our kit was occupying a section of the press office just behind Channel 4's production area and we flopped down on a couple of chairs dividing the two.

'Ah, the blondes,' said a voice. 'I've been looking for both of you.' It was the young, glamorous Kennel Club press officer. Word about the huskies must have got out quickly. Anna shifted in her chair and nervously stroked Molly.

'They were hoping you could do the Get Fit with Fido interview with Clare Balding this evening, before the close and the final montage of the first day.'

She was wearing a headset and carrying a clipboard, and looked perky and shiny, which made us feel worn out and old. She was also very efficient and from the way the request was delivered, it was obvious that only a 'yes' would do. If we wanted to make the Channel 4 show, it would have to be now or never.

The two of us tried to look alert and eager instead of totally unprepared. We had assumed the Balding item would be on the second day, when our own show was out of the way and we'd had time to do our research. That way we would have been fresh and enthusiastic as opposed to frayed and ill informed.

'Great,' we said in unison. 'Lead the way.'

Unlike our makeshift shack hidden down one end of the press office, Clare Balding's temporary TV studio was sumptuous – a stage with lighting rigging, two cameras and a big comfy 'on set' leather chair. Clare was seated in it when we arrived, speaking into the camera. To the side of her were three guest chairs. A vet was seated on one of them and Clare swung round to engage him in an in-depth discussion on breeding issues.

A childlike production assistant, in the obligatory headset, guided the two of us with Molly and Matilda to the side of the set.

'You'll be on those chairs.' She pointed at the vacant seats, and whispered, 'One of us will take you onto the stage when they go to the next VT.' That's short for video transmission.

We nodded. Then I looked closely at Anna. It wouldn't be unkind to say she appeared unkempt. Grains of sand from the husky ring could be seen around her neck and at almost 7 p.m. any signs of make-up had completely disappeared. If she looked rough, what on earth must I have looked like? I'd set out from London 12 hours previously and since then hadn't had time to look in the mirror.

'Excuse me,' I called in a loud whisper to the production assistant, thinking she must surely have been on work experience. 'Could you tell us where the make-up wagon is?'

She looked blank. 'Oh, yes. It's out in the car park but I'm afraid they've packed up.'

I swung back to face Anna.

'We can't be seen in this state,' I hissed. 'We both look like grubs. Our aim is to put glamour back into the dog world. Not frighten the viewers.'

'Oh Lord, you're right,' said Anna, who was watching the interview with the vet with interest. 'Clare's got loads of slap on. She's going to make us look anaemic.'

'And old,' I added.

Neither of us had our handbags, since we had been herded up in such a hurry, hence no make-up and no hair brush. I was grappling with the idea of how I would explain my appearance to my ever-critical, viewing mother when another ghastly thought entered my head.

'What is Get Fit with Fido?' I hissed at Anna.

'I'm not really sure,' she said, sheepishly. 'It's a campaign launched by the Kennel Club but I haven't had a chance to crib up on it yet. I'd planned on doing the research over break-fast tomorrow.'

'What?' I spat. 'You mean we're about to go on national television, devoid of make-up and with no idea of what we're talking about?'

Anna bent over suddenly and began hanging like a rag doll, shaking her head from side to side. I thought, 'Surely she can't have fainted.'

'Do this,' she said from under a mop of long blonde hair. 'It helps lift the hair if a brush isn't available. It gives it body. Equivalent to a root lift.'

I dropped forward to touch my toes and swung my head from side to side.

'Excuse me,' came a quiet voice from behind us. 'May I fit your mics?' The sound boy also looked like an infant. Are television crews like policemen and beginning to look younger and younger?

Our signature wrap-around dresses were a bad choice for a microphone fitting but after a great deal of fussing about, it was agreed we would hold the sound packs in our hands. Once seated, we were told, we should hide them down the back of our chairs.

Never have we felt more ill equipped for a television appear-ance than we did that evening at Crufts. Radio may be treated like the poor relation, but it matters not a jot how tired you look. If you're caught on the hop and haven't prepped your interview, you can actually read up on it while the programme is going out. We liked to think our listeners always pictured us as blonde perfection. On live TV there can be no cheating because there is no place to hide.

'Now remember,' I said to Anna, 'it's all about energy. Energy, energy, energy. As long as we're not dull it will be okay.'

'Yes,' repeated Anna, unconvinced. 'Energy, energy, energy.'

Matilda looked up at us and yawned.

During a break for VT we were led onto the set by another toddler, shook hands with Clare and sat down next to the vet. Molly lay neatly by Anna's feet; Matilda sat like a disgruntled Margaret Rutherford, facing directly towards the camera with her underbite showing. The cameraman whistled at her. 'Oh please don't do that,' I thought.

The passing public were able to stand and watch from a distance and a few lingered to take photos of Clare on their phones, but most, by now, were heading for home.

Clare turned to the camera, looked at the autocue and introduced us by saying, 'They call themselves the Barking Blondes ...' which I felt was slightly dismissive, but Anna and the vet smiled, so I guess it sounded okay. To be honest, I didn't really hear much of what she said because I was so panicked by how we were expected to respond.

I'd also just caught sight of the two of us on a monitor positioned on the floor. Our dream of looking like the Trinny and Susannah of the dog world was shattered immediately. Anna was looking more like Worzel Gummidge to my Aunt Sally. We looked exhausted.

'So tell us about Get Fit with Fido,' I heard Clare say.

The plan was to let Anna lead since her knowledge far outweighs mine and she actually knows what she's talking about whereas I'm all hot air. But the bossy leader in me couldn't stay quiet, even when I was lacking information. Years of working in radio had trained me to fill a silence. Consequently, we both took deep breaths and blurted out a stream of details at the same time.

'Look at a fat owner and you will find a fat dog,' Anna began.

Alarm bells went off in my head. At the BBC, the word fat was never encouraged because it could be thought to be patronizing, so immediately I took it upon myself to recover the situation.

'Well, not all large dogs have large owners,' I started, not really knowing where I was going with this, 'but let's face it, we could all eat less and exercise more.'

Clare looked at the autocue and the vet lent back in his chair in an attempt to remove himself from any part of this.

Anna resumed, 'Jo and I both do yoga and, do you know, there's a position called face down dog.'

'Yes,' I chipped in. 'We really can learn from the animals ...

This inanity continued until a low growling noise came from under Anna's chair. Molly had clocked one of the Siberian huskies walking past and obviously wanted to prove she was queen of the castle because she was on the set and the husky wasn't. She gave another low, just audible to us, long growl.

'Quiet, ducky,' Anna said.

Clare and the vet just looked at us. Both had obviously assumed that Anna was talking to me.

'Ducky!' I thought. 'Oh Lord, they'll think we're lesbians. As will the viewers. Never mind, I suppose it's a thriving market.'

One of the toddler people was standing behind the camera doing wind-up gestures, indicating it was time to throw forward to another VT. We shook hands again with the vet and started to tiptoe off the set. Clare lent over and whispered to us, 'My God, you can talk, the pair of you, but loads of energy. Thank you.'

The monitor on the floor was playing out the VT montage of that day's events at Crufts. I watched with horror as the final lingering shot was of Anna flying head first into the sand and revealing the whitest of white knickers. Thankfully, she was kneeling down pacifying a disgruntled Molly and hadn't seen it, but no doubt our phones would be full of texts from London.

Back in the empty press office, our own producer, the wonderful Mel, had arrived. He had plugged in the ISDN line, as well as our own BBC computers, and unpacked the microphones and headsets. Everyone else had left for the night. Three security guards lingered by the doors, waiting to escort our so far phantom guests into and out of the building. All we could hear were the cleaners polishing the floors and the locking of doors. After that, for a while, it seemed as though we were the only people left in the massive NEC building.

'Right, there's an hour before we go to air,' said Mel. 'Who have we got in the running order?'

'We did have a Marilyn lookalike with a toy poodle,' said Anna, 'but he hasn't confirmed, and other than him, we'll just have to wait and see who's still awake and willing to come back after their suppers.'

Mel looked suitably unimpressed.

'I've brought you a couple of Red Bulls,' he said, chucking us the cans. 'We should log on and see if they're ready for a sound check back at base.'

I took a slug of the Red Bull. I'd never drunk one before and it was much needed. We were shattered but the biggest event for us this day had yet to happen. We had a four-hour radio show ahead of us.

'Oh this is quite nice,' said Anna, slugging back the whole can.

I put in my BBC password and logged on. An email from George leapt on to my screen with the message: LOOK WHERE I'VE BEEN. The attachment revealed a picture of an unfamiliar kitchen, and George kneeling in a playpen surrounded by five bulldog puppies. My heart leapt. They were beautiful, about nine weeks old and, unlike Matilda, were all red. I called Anna over.

'Look at these,' I said. 'Do you recognize that kitchen?'

'Nope,' she answered. 'Oh, they look adorable. Whose are they?' I had no idea.

'My internet connection has frozen,' said Anna, banging at the keyboard. 'I was in the middle of researching the history of the greyhound.' She gave an almighty burp and her eyes had started to roll.

'Oops, pardon ... I thought I might be able to pad out the programme with some research on the lurcher but all I can tell you is that the greyhound is one of the oldest breeds and is mentioned in the Bible.'

'Anna, your eyes are rolling,' I said in a panic. 'You shouldn't have drunk that energy drink on top of all our coffees.'

'It's okay,' she said, standing up. 'I'll practise a bit of yoga, since there's nobody here.'

With that she tucked her dress into her tights, went over to one of the massive columns and started doing handstands against it. Mel looked at me and grinned.

'She shouldn't have drunk the whole can,' he said. 'I think the world has seen enough of her upside down for a bit. You know there was a shot of her knickers on Channel 4 tonight?'

'I know,' I replied. 'Say nothing.'

Suddenly, the sound of a single pair of footsteps could be heard, echoing across the piazza. Behind us, the door to the press office opened and a voice asked, 'Is this the right place for the radio show?'

Anna returned her feet to the ground with a thud at the same time as Mel and I jumped up to greet Pete Wedderburn. Pete is the vet columnist from the *Telegraph* and had arrived 30 minutes before transmission time to give us support. This was such a relief. I'd never met him before but I hugged him as I would my father. If all else failed, and we were stranded in the empty exhibition hall without guests, we could invite Pete to take questions from the listeners. That, along with some doggy tracks, would fill an hour.

'Anna, I've just seen a clip of you on Channel 4 ...' Pete started to say.

'Girls, can you sit behind your mics,' Mel broke in. 'We're live in a few minutes.'

We went to take our places at the makeshift broadcast desk – just two minutes before we went to air. Anna had put her headphones on over her tousled hair, leaving it sticking up like Lene Lovich. In front of her was half a page of script on the history of the greyhound.

Our loyal listeners, we hoped, were waiting for this momentous occasion. An engineer, back at base, was telling Mel how many texts of good luck we had received and, worryingly, that some of senior management had stayed behind to listen in.

With 90 seconds to go, the doors to the press office opened again and there, filling the doorway, was the biggest dog we had ever seen. Covered in long brown fur it was the size of a pony and was standing almost to attention. Its owner looked as fit as the dog. They made a handsome pair.

'It's Pen!' shouted Anna, pulling off her headphones and running over to hug him.

This was the uber fit, ex-marine Pen Farthing and his dog Max. We had contacted them weeks ago but received no reply. Pen runs a charity called Nowzad, which rescues dogs from Aghanistan, and he had flown Max back to Blighty to live with him. For a floundering running order at a live broadcast, this was manna from heaven indeed.

At precisely 10 p.m. our familiar theme tune *Barking at the Moon*, sung by the Jive Aces, started to play through our headphones.

'Mics up,' whispered the engineer.

'Good evening and welcome to *Barking at the Moon*, coming to you live tonight from Crufts at the Birmingham NEC,' I began. 'Woof! Woof'!'

Then it was Anna's turn, slightly breathless.

'We have a whole host of doggy guests turning up to speak to you tonight, including a war veteran and his dog from Afghanistan and the *Telegraph*'s own vet to take calls on health ...'

The live, historical broadcast from Crufts went out without a hitch. Goodwill from a stream of enthusiastic guests, along with excellent production from Mel, meant we filled four hours from an almost empty exhibition centre until 2 a.m. Even management must have been pleased.

Nothing, not even cans of Red Bull, could keep us awake that night. Back at the on-site hotel, we walked our exhausted dogs, played back the events of the day and retired to bed just as dawn was breaking over Birmingham. The final image in my mind, before falling into a deep and welcome sleep, was of George in a playpen surrounded by puppies.

Back in London, Big George's basement flat was my first port of call.

'Hurrah! Hurrah!' he shouted through the entry phone. Once inside, we jogged down the stairs and, when she saw him standing at his door, Matilda hurtled down the corridor and flung herself at him. I was curious to know what he'd been up to. I'd not received any communication from him on my second day at Crufts. To go from receiving calls and texts regularly, often hourly, to hearing nothing was quite alarming.

Among the familiar chaos of his flat, I noticed that the bed was covered in sweaters and shirts, most of which I'd never seen before.

'I've been back home and collected more stuff,' he said, taking in my gaze. 'Oh and look.' He pointed at two plastic 'humane' mousetraps against the skirting board.

This was the first time in our entire relationship that he had ever voluntarily mentioned returning to his family home.

Ignoring the topic of mousetraps, I moved a big, cable pullover, handknitted, out the way and sat down on the corner of his bed. These items of clothing, I realized, were fresh from somewhere near Milton Keynes, and so, presumably, was he.

'I called in on Anne Marie,' he said, as though reading my thoughts. 'I've bought a puppy.'

I was stunned.

Anne Marie is a bulldog breeder and her bitch was Matilda's grandmother. She and her husband, Jim, are two of the kindest and loveliest people I have ever met in the dog world, and they live just outside Milton Keynes. We had met them once, early on, when I'd been looking for advice about Matilda's feeding. Nobody knew more about the eccentricities of bulldogs than Anne Marie.

I was trying to take all this in. It must have been their kitchen, then, that was featured in the picture with the puppies in the playpen.

George got out his phone and started to scroll through pictures.

'Look,' he said, showing me the image of three, 10-week-old puppies. Two were brindle and the other was red and white. They were all bundled into his arms and he was smiling into the camera.

'I've been given first choice of these three bitches,' he said, grinning from ear to ear.

'Oh my God, George,' I said. 'When did you decide this? They are beautiful.'

Not only was I taken completely by surprise at his decision to buy a puppy, but also that he had done all this without me.

'Anne Marie and I have been in discussion for some time,' he said, not looking me in the eye. 'I just needed to take time off to see them for myself.'

This was weird. He was beginning to talk in the first person as opposed to 'us'. The puppy was, obviously, very much going to be *his* dog and that made me feel strange.

'Don't choose a brindle,' I said, somewhat bossily. 'The red is far more attractive.'

He put the phone down on the bed, picked up one of his guitars and started to strum. His guitar face always annoyed me – it was impossible to penetrate his expression, or to hold a sensible conversation.

'Honestly, George,' I continued. 'Brindles are quite common. I would definitely opt for the red. And can we call her Mabel?'

I loved the name Mabel. My nan had been called Mabel. He continued to strum.

'I haven't decided on which one yet, and I want to name her myself. She'll be ready to collect this week.'

He had his guitar face on and I needed to think. I left Matilda sitting by his side, listening to music, and walked the four minutes back to my flat. This should have been a day to celebrate. George getting his own dog would mean more independence from me. Puppies are time consuming and his days would be full of training and feeding. Not being able to see Matilda wouldn't matter to him quite so much.

However, it was in my nature to want to take some control over his acquisition. George always asked my advice on everything, so why didn't he act on it now?

During the next few days, whenever I had a spare moment, I would shop for the new puppy. Everything I knew about puppy rearing I had learned from George. But I also knew he would leave everything to the last minute and have nothing prepared for her homecoming.

Anna came up trumps by filling her car with products from clients, such as puppy pads, toys and an indestructible bed. She was as excited about the imminent arrival as I was. I retrieved Matilda's old baby gate from the back of my wardrobe and placed it in readiness with the other stuff.

George had no idea that we had rallied round. In keeping with his new-found independence, he had insisted on going to Anne Marie's to collect the dog on his own. Part of me wondered if this was because he was going to call in to his family home on the way.

I waited in London for his return. Matilda and I sat by our front door, eager for his text. It arrived just as it was getting dark. A message accompanied by a picture of a red and white puppy: HERE SHE IS. COME ON DOWN TO MEET HER. HER NAME IS MABEL.

CHAPTER 6

'That day, they seemed to be making all of Primrose Hill happy.'

I've heard parents say that no two offspring are alike and I guess the same can be said of puppies. My only experience of bulldogs, up until Mabel's arrival, had been Matilda and I'd assumed her behaviour to be representative of the breed – stubborn but quiet, docile and affectionate. From her early days, Matilda was left for short periods and we would always return to find her curled up and asleep. She adapted very quickly to living in the restrictive space of an inner-city studio flat.

Mabel was a distant cousin to Matilda, they apparently shared the same father, but they couldn't have been more different. To start with, Mabel was a redhead in every sense – fiery and impulsive. She had one of the most appealing faces ever to be bred in a bullie. Two frown lines gave her an expression that was constantly quizzical or concerned. She had a beautiful, round-shaped head, not squashed flat like many bulldogs, and the wrinkle on her nose was not too thick. Her legs were long and coltish. She was cute and very healthy and as affectionate as any bulldog. However, Mabel had the personality of a terrier.

'Meet my new girlfriend,' George said as I fell to my knees and scooped her up from his kitchen floor. 'What a little cracker! She sat on my lap all the way down the M1.'

'That must have been quite a sight,' I thought, 'as well as totally unlawful.'

I was still coming to terms with the realization that he had spent weeks negotiating with Anne Marie, completed the transaction and chosen Mabel without needing any advice from me. Decisions as big as this we had previously made together. And yet, as he watched me indulge in her cuteness, there was nothing possessive about his behaviour. He had delivered her back to London for me to fall in love with. Job done.

Matilda, a little curious, briefly sniffed about the new puppy, then nonchalantly retreated to her den. Always the perfect dog owner, George coaxed her out from under the bed by making a fuss of her and deliberately walking her round the block. That way she didn't feel the puppy had ousted her from his affections and it also meant I got to be alone with Mabel.

We stared at each other with mutual interest and I prayed there and then that she and I between us could supply George with all the affection he needed.

Looking about his flat, I noticed that he had made no attempt to prepare for her arrival other than putting up Matilda's baby gate between his kitchen and his bedsitting room. Her bed was a few of his old sweaters and her bowls were odd dishes he'd found in cupboards – so very different from the over-indulged Matilda. All the rest of the puppy paraphernalia was waiting in my car, supplied either by Anna or made up of Matilda's cast-offs.

As I waited for George and Matilda to return, I wandered into the bathroom. Mabel followed. She was energetic and inquisitive, and determined never to miss out. The bathroom was in its usual state of chaos – music magazines along with T-shirts littered across the floor, a bath that had never been cleaned and brandy bottles lying on their side.

On the sink rested the pink hand towel that George always left out for me and now, next to it, was a smaller, brand new candy striped one. This he must have bought for Mabel. My heart surged.

It was Mabel's first day away from her mother, in her new home, and so we decided to offer total support by all spending the night together. George and I were in the bed, Matilda under it and Mabel on her makeshift pile of sweaters, behind the baby gate, on the kitchen floor.

All was peaceful until around dawn. Then she started to whimper. I froze, nudged George and we braced ourselves, praying for her to go to sleep. She didn't. The whimpers got louder until eventually she was barking, proper loud barks of distress. It was the early hours of Sunday morning and we could hear Ian, the caretaker, moving about in the flat next door.

'Leave her,' said George. 'If we go to her, we're on a hiding to nothing.'

The barks started to get more frantic.

'She'll wake the whole block,' I said. 'It's only 7.30.'

Neither of us knew what to do. Matilda had never barked. I didn't think bulldogs were a barking breed. Tiny Mabel had the bark of a fully grown dog and she was clearly distressed. A door banged in the apartment above.

'Oh Christ,' said George, getting up. 'I'm going to have to go in and pick her up.'

Throwing off the bed covers, he swung his legs over the side of the bed and sat with his head in his hands. The barks got louder.

He walked over to the kitchenette, stepped over the baby gate, lifted her up to his chest and sat back down on the bed. Matilda's nose came out from under the bed. She looked grumpy at being woken, but on seeing Mabel, she retreated back into her den. Mabel had stopped the noise the moment she was held and now fell asleep in George's massive arms. We had committed the number-one mistake. I was feeling anxious.

'It'll be all right,' I said, sensing George's concern. 'We just need to go out for short bursts and leave her. If she barks, she barks. That's what they say in the books. Eventually, she'll stop.'

None of that sounded convincing.

We got dressed, fed each dog separately, laid down fresh newspaper in the kitchen, placed Mabel on it, shut the baby gate and prepared to go out. Matilda was on her lead, straining to get outside, but we had only got as far as the front door when the barking recommenced.

'Let's go,' I said to George, pushing him and Matilda through the door and shutting it behind us. We stood frozen on the other side of it as the barks got louder and louder. Sounds of people moving around could now be heard from the surrounding apartments as Mabel's distress echoed around the block.

'Hell,' cursed George, unlocking the door. 'We can't leave her like this.'

Against all the rules, we went back in and I picked up Mabel. George sat on the bed, looking scared. I'd never seen him like that, but neither of us had any idea what to do.

'Right,' I said, trying to think things through in my mind. 'We're not going to be able to train her to be left on her own when people are at home for the day. Or they'll complain. We'll have to leave her alone to bark when everyone's out at work.'

I'd never seen him appear so vulnerable. George always came to the rescue of whatever dilemma I found myself in. Looking at him now, he seemed defeated. He was rocking a sleeping Mabel in his arms, distracted and searching my face for a solution.

'We'll work this out,' I said to him, totally unconvinced. 'I'm taking Matilda round the block. You stay here in case she wakes up.'

We were committing the ultimate no no in dog training, allowing Mabel to have the upper hand. But what else could we have done? I didn't even call Anna because I knew what advice she would have offered. We were making the proverbial rod for our own back. However, given the circumstances, there was nothing else we could do.

I led Matilda out of the flat, closed the door, turned round and walked slap bang into Ian. He was standing, hands on hips, staring angrily at George's flat. His eyes were red and so was his face. It looked as though he had been holding his breath.

'What the hell is going on?' he demanded.

I was lost for words, so I said nothing.

'What have you two got in there? That wasn't Matilda I heard barking. Is there another dog in there?'

Oh no, a sense of what was about to occur dawned on me. Surely, he wasn't going to ban her? George was his friend. He let Matilda come and go without ever objecting.

'It's a puppy,' I said quietly. 'It's George's new puppy. She's just a bit disorientated.'

'Get it out. It can't stay,' said Ian. 'No dogs. There are no dogs allowed in this block. It's in the lease.'

I felt sick.

'Matilda's okay because she doesn't live here.' He was now puce. 'If anyone from the managing agent's learns there's a dog living in this building, I'll get the sack.'

Rigid with anger, he continued to stand there, staring at me and preventing me from moving down the corridor, so I was forced to retreat towards George's flat. I scrabbled about with my keys and let myself back in.

George had heard all of the exchange. He was standing in the middle of the room, holding Mabel, with the same pleading look in his eyes – a cry for help that had a vulnerability I had never seen in him before.

Why had neither of us thought this through? During the planning, the choosing and then the bringing home, it had never occurred to him that a puppy wouldn't be welcome. But then why would George have thought of needing permission? Matilda's arrival in London had been considered a major acquisition and caused no problem with my apartment.

My block, it appears, is one of a few in the neighbourhood to allow dogs. Also, my position was different because I owned my flat, so if ever I was questioned, I had some kind of bargaining power. George had none. He answered to a landlord.

'Oh hell,' I said, sitting back down on his bed. 'What are we going to do?'

'Nothing,' replied George. 'I'll make sure nobody sees me bringing a dog in and out of the block and she must never be left to bark.'

'Aren't you going to speak to Ian?' I asked, thinking this must be one of the classic examples of sticking your head in the sand.

'He hasn't spoken to me,' George said. 'So I'm not defying him. As far as he's concerned, he told all this to you and he's expecting me to act on his request.'

The most obvious solution would have been for Mabel to live with me. It would have been hideously overcrowded with two dogs, but it could have worked. However, George would never have asked for this and I was definitely not going to suggest it. The whole plan had been to have a dog in his own home. As well as something for him to love, he knew Mabel was always going to draw me down to his end of the street.

Matilda started pulling me towards the door. She was confused and in need of a pee. Since the puppy had appeared in this flat, everything in her world had become frantic.

Ian had gone from the corridor and as we left the block, she seemed, for the first time, relieved to be heading back up the street to my place, where she was always queen of the castle.

So Mabel's life with George began in a very unsatisfactory way. What should have been, for him, a loving and affectionate distraction became another reason for secrecy. She was a stowaway, living in a mansion block, illegally. Checking always to make certain Ian was out of sight, George would hide Mabel under his cashmere winter coat and smuggle her into and out of his building.

Once she was in the street and free, she galloped by his side, mainly sideways, and looking over her shoulder, in the true style of a bulldog. Naturally, they became inseparable.

Apart from the four hours when he was at the BBC on air, Mabel was with George. Big man, little dog, they were a familiar sight in Marylebone High Street and on all the routes into Soho. His obvious pleasure at having her was marred only by the stress of smuggling her into and out of his home throughout the day.

We organized his absence at work with military precision. George would have Matilda and Mabel with him every evening. I would drive into work, park my car outside the BBC and present my late show. We were expected, at the end of my show, to overlap and chat for a moment or two about what he would be covering in his show, which followed mine. However, we skipped that and I would simply sign off and be on my way. George, meanwhile, walked the dogs to my car, put them in it and headed for the studio. We would rush past each other in reception, going in opposite directions. It meant that between me signing off and him taking over, the girls were left alone in my car for just two minutes.

For the whole of that period, those nights when Mabel was in the car with Matilda were the happiest I can remember. I would walk outside Broadcasting House at 2 a.m. and in the lamplight I'd see both dogs huddled for warmth on the driver's seat – one large white head, the other little and red, and both peering through the steering wheel. It was the best bit of my day.

We would drive through the abandoned streets to my flat, where I would fall asleep, with both dogs, adrift on the platform bed. Later, George would let himself quietly into the flat and collect his puppy before smuggling her back into his place. As elaborate as this may sound, it was a routine that worked, so we never knew if Mabel could cope with being left alone, because she never was!

The only day the routine altered was on a Friday, which was George's night off. I did a breakfast show on the Saturday morning and so George and Mabel would leave me to sleep on Friday nights while they partied in the West End. George would always give me an alarm call at 5 a.m., no matter where he was or in what state, but usually as they were both heading home to bed.

To our friends and colleagues this seemed such a rigmarole, but we didn't mind. It was fun and, for a while, it worked.

'I'm worried about the extent Mabel walks,' said Anna to me one day as we were in a cab on the way Channel 5. She's still very young but George expects her to walk from Marylebone to Soho and back every day.'

'Sometimes twice a day if you count dinner at Bar Italia,' I added. 'Are you going to have the courage to tell George? I'm not.'

'No way,' admitted Anna. 'I wouldn't dare. He's very dogmatic with her – no pun intended. He pulls her away from Molly when they meet, as though she's in danger.' I'd noticed this, but had never commented.

The Barking Blondes were about to make their first appearance on Channel 5's daytime Gaby Logan programme. We had been booked for an item on canine Christmas gifts. Stuffed in the cab with us, as well as Molly and Matilda, both wearing antlers, were bags of merchandise for a studio display. Anna had done her homework.

Channel 5 is at the top of Whiteleys Shopping Centre and dogs are banned, so we were given VIP attention, met by a floor assistant and escorted through the concourse. Both of us are anarchic enough still to love breaking rules where dog areas are concerned. There is nothing better than security guards having to watch and let the girls walk by. Molly and Matilda both appeared to sense the concession and trotted through the crowds of appreciative shoppers with their heads held high. A couple of fans shouted 'Woof! Woof!' which gave us Dutch courage to enter an as yet unknown TV environment.

The massive office of Princess Productions was full of young, aspirational people, who all looked up as we burst through their doors, leading two dogs wearing antlers. Daytime television is a zoo. All of human life passes through its doors. We had already experienced it with a couple of appearances on ITV's *This Morning*, and loved it. Channel 5 had the same vibe. Researchers and crew left their posts to enthuse over Molly and Matilda, leaving us wondering, yet again, why dogs aren't allowed more often into the work place. If someone in the back room was shoving antihistamine down their throats to stave off an allergy, we never heard about it.

We were taken to make-up, and, no word of a lie, this has to be one of our favourite rooms in the world. The Channel 5 make-up girls host the best party in town. Six make-up chairs face a long mirror. Three of them were occupied by Osmond brothers. On seeing us, all three leapt out of their chairs to come and make a fuss of the dogs.

That stopped us in our tracks and we listened to their enthusiastic words in amazement and delight. Apparently, they loved dogs, had grown up with them from childhood. We sat ourselves in chairs on either side, and they tried to recall the names and breeds of all their past pets. Anna was nodding and smiling, at the same time as being concerned about the amount of eyebrow powder being painted on her face. I was more intrigued to see if they all had their own hair. Gossip, make-up and the Osmonds – we were in heaven.

Anna's true talent at selecting and explaining gadgets, most of which had been trialled by Molly, as well as her knowledge of what doggy products were available, was invaluable in these set-ups. I would just leave her to chat with the researchers as they dressed the set, in full confidence that when we were asked, she would have every bit of detail in her head. This is what made us useful to consumer features.

We were taken to the green room to wait for the show to start, and Gaby Logan came in to greet us. Strikingly attractive and dressed in a green Marc Jacobs blouse, she headed straight for the dogs and they lapped it up. This was a real lesson for us on how to treat guests. Back at the BBC, due to the manic nature of our own radio programme, we often didn't meet contributors until we were actually on air, seated in the studio and about to start the interview. Gaby came to meet her guests prior to transmission, and we noticed how much more relaxed everybody was, and how that generated a party atmosphere. We decided that, from then on, we would adopt the same routine and respect our contributors more.

On this occasion, she had certainly relaxed us, not only with her warm and giggly personality, but also because she loved dogs. She described her boxer, Sidney, and how she and husband Kenny were trying to train him without much luck. Anna began to offer advice and I could see Gaby realizing that we weren't a pair of vacuous dog lovers and some expertise lay behind what we did.

On this Channel 5 show, the cameras were also in the green room and focused on the guests as they waited to go on. It's a ploy Jonathan Ross uses and is a great way of trailing what's coming up. The Osmonds were on first and already seated in the studio. We were not on until later and so remained in the green room along with fellow contributor Amy Childs from *The Only Way Is Essex*. Another avid dog lover, Amy enthused over the girls while a member of her entourage rubbed moisturizer into her legs. I caught Anna's eyes – in fact, it was hard not to, her eyebrows were so dark – and we knew exactly what each other was thinking.

Unlike the episode with Clare Balding, we were completely in our comfort zone. Plastered in make-up and surrounded by reality television folk, this was a nice place to be.

Once the show was on air, we could see and hear it via a monitor in front of us. The cameraman in the green room swung the camera round to where Molly and Matilda were sitting, antlers still on their heads.

'Coming up,' said Gaby, 'the Barking Blondes take a look at a doggy Christmas and Amy Childs helps us to keep fit,' and onto the screen bounced a cutaway of the girls and next to them, just in vision, Amy's well-mosturized legs. Then the shot was back on Gaby in the studio.

Anna's phone, on silent, began to vibrate in her bag with the arrival of a text. We were off camera for the next ten minutes so she reached down to read it.

'Oh it's from Rupert,' she said eagerly. 'He says "NICE LEGS GIRL!"'

Oh well, if Rupert To The Rescue thought Amy's long, tanned, moisturized legs belonged to one of us, let him. I was interested to see their friendship had become so informal. Loyal of him to be watching us on daytime telly.

Where was George I wondered? He wouldn't know Channel 5 if it landed on his head. Hopefully, he had smuggled Mabel out of his flat for the day and they were pounding the familiar streets of Soho.

'Coming up,' shouted the cameraman, 'end of part one. Everybody in position, please.'

Anna had lifted Molly on to her lap, where she sat in her travelling-on-the-bus position, like an upturned table. It's very funny to observe. The camera was on the two of them in the cutaway as Gaby wound up with, 'And still to come ... the Barking Blondes look at a barking good yuletide.'

The camera moved from Molly and Anna to a shot of Matilda, snoring on the floor next to Amy Childs' massive platform Christian Louboutin, gold-platformed shoes.

'Rest everybody, we're in a commercial break,' shouted the cameraman.

Anna picked up her phone after it once again vibrated.

'Look at this,' she said, showing me another text from Rupert. It read: WOW, DIG THE SHOES!

'Does he really think either you or I could walk in those?' I laughed. 'He seems very attentive.'

'He was round last night giving Molly some acupuncture,' Anna said. 'Just to tune her up for today. He gave me a foot massage.'

Before I could respond, they were sticking mics on us. This is always a bit of a procedure because, as we both like to wear dresses, the cords have to be threaded down our bras, often with the assistance of the sound engineer. Over the months, we have become quite adept at it, but occasionally the fiasco is performed in a public space, such as a green room. I watched aghast as a meatball fell out of Anna's bra on to the floor, where Matilda immediately swiped and swallowed it.

'What was that?' asked the sound man, still grappling with Anna's dress.

'Don't ask,' I replied. 'But it's the difference between the girls sitting nicely on the set or running amok.'

Anna looked at me, a little fearfully.

'That was the last meatball,' she whispered. 'Oh Lord, I hope they behave.'

So did I. Our dogs work on a reward basis. If they sit nicely and quietly, they know that, at the end of it, they will get a treat. Anna's meatballs have got us through numerous media events by encouraging the girls to behave beautifully. Now, our first time on Channel 5, we had to hope they would succeed without the meaty enticements.

We were to be the last item on the programme, so we sat through Amy Childs' engaging chat about sports bras and were led into the studio during the following commercial break.

Gorgeous Gaby remained in her high-backed, presenter's chair and we were invited to sit alongside on the sofa, still warm, we imagined, from the posteriors of the Osmonds. Both dogs were encouraged to sit up on the sofa with us. Matilda, the most belligerent, usually obliged because she could scent a Swedish meatball on Anna's person. Until she realized there wasn't one, I hoped she would remain in shot, quietly. Molly, always camera savvy, was tucked in next to Anna, looking straight down the lens.

Spread out in front of us was the array of Christmas doggy gifts, sorted by Anna, but to my surprise, a plate of homemade dog biscuits had appeared among them. These were obviously to promote a *Bake Your Own Fido Snack* cookery book. An enthusiastic researcher must have baked them – neither of us would ever bring food onto the set in front of the dogs, unless, of course, it was in the shape of hidden treats.

Anna, Molly and Matilda all clocked the biscuits at the same moment as I did.

'Excuse me.' Anna waved at a member of the crew. 'Would you mind taking the biscuits off the table or the dogs will be distracted.'

'Going live in 5, 4, 3, 2, 1,' said the floor manager, and waved his hand under the camera. As he shouted 'Action' so the biscuits were rapidly removed out of shot and taken off the set by an adept props guy. Molly's eyes followed their exit.

'Welcome back,' said Gaby, 'and let me introduce you to two of the most dog enthusiastic ...' and she was off with her introduction.

Something about that first show made us relax and enjoy the item. As Gaby enthused and demonstrated each gift, so Anna described beautifully its function and availability. The crew, along with a small live studio audience, were encouraged to laugh and react throughout. They seemed to do it spontaneously. They were enjoying it as much as we were.

So when at the very end of the slot, Gaby Logan looked at Molly and said, 'I've been told that you are a champion doggy dancer, Molly, and we're hoping you will end with a little demonstration,' both Anna and I were chuffed.

The floor manager gestured for Anna and Molly to stand up and move centre stage as the opening bars of Little Eva's *Locomotion* began to play out. Gaby Logan and I, along with the studio audience and the viewers at home, settled down to watch this party piece.

Anna started to gyrate her hips in a hula-hoop fashion. Generally, this would encourage Molly to stand on her back legs, turn circles and join in. Unfortunately, Molly's attention was still drawn towards the plate of biscuits that had been rapidly removed to somewhere at the back of the studio. Knowing there were no meaty morsels on Anna's person, she had absolutely no intention of jumping through legs, especially when there were biscuits hidden somewhere nearby.

The viewing nation watched as Anna did a dotted skip and a pirouette, like an idiot, while Molly stood stock still. Removing her stare from down the camera lens, she obligingly did one jump through Anna's open legs, then turned and trotted off the set, past Gaby to the green room. Little Eva was continuing to play out as Gaby turned to the camera and wound up the programme.

'Well, that's it,' she said, grinning. 'Let's hope we find Molly before tomorrow, when we shall be back with none other than Myleene Klass.'

The closing titles came up over Anna dancing alone like 'Betty no mates' while Gaby lent back in her chair, laughing. The final shot was of Anna running in despair through the audience, shouting, 'Molls, Molls, come on nood ... where are you?'

Confused as to whether we had been a disaster or a success, I was led from the set, with Matilda in tow, and across the floor to be introduced to the executive producer. She shook hands with me and hugged Gaby, who in turn hugged a distraught Anna.

'I love these two,' Gaby told the exec. 'Don't you think we should make this a regular item?'

And that's what happened. Molly's cunning and belligerence earned us a regular slot on the daytime Channel 5 show, for as long as it ran..

Our schedule had now become even more demanding, with Channel 5, the radio show and episodes of the Sky series still to film. Any spare time left over at the weekend was taken up with personal appearances at dog shows.

Mabel was proving to be a winning distraction for George. Her unique terrier-like energy and litheness meant she kept up with him, even as a puppy, on all his urban walks. She was still living the life of a stowaway, though. George continued to smuggle her in and out of his building.

One afternoon I needed to drop Matilda off at George's while I went to do a voiceover in Soho. I'd called him earlier and he hadn't replied. I figured I'd let myself in, leave Matilda and then collect her on the way back. We both had the key to each other's flat, so there was a lot of dropping off of dogs and collecting them throughout the day.

As I walked up the steps to George's block I bumped into Ian, who was Brassoing the front railings. I hadn't seen him since the first morning of Mabel's barking and now I was embarrassed and didn't know what to say.

'Is George in?' I asked, knowing Ian watched all exits and entrances on his CCTV.

'Reckon he is', he answered. 'He has been avoiding me. If he still has that puppy in there I'll have to report him.'

I looked him in the eye and took a deep breath.

'Ian, please don't kick the dog out. Please don't stitch him up. You can see how much George loves Matilda and now he has a puppy of his own.'

Ian stood his ground, staring into my eyes, not moving.

I continued, 'You know the situation, Ian, or you must have guessed. He left his wife for me. I am always busy. I'm never here. He needs this puppy to love.'

Then I burst into tears.

By talking so unguarded to this ex-squaddie caretaker, I'd summed up the situation that, up until now, George and I had not dared to define. Ian, embarrassed, looked down at the floor and took his time before he spoke.

'Mate, it's not up to me. It's written in the lease. It's my head that will roll, not his. I've told him that the dog can't stay and he's promised me it will be out tomorrow.'

I nodded, disbelievingly

He patted my shoulder, screwed the top back on his Brasso and walked off.

I was going to have to report this conversation to George. Matilda was jumping up and down at his door, eager to see him. I let myself in. The flat wasn't empty. Lounging on the sofa, strumming his guitar, was George, and standing with Mabel in his arms was a young, very good-looking schoolboy.

George immediately sat up and laid down the guitar. Matilda rushed over to him.

'This is my grandson,' he said, slightly flustered .

I took in the scene. I'd never until this moment met a member of George's family and wasn't at all sure what role I was supposed to play. So far, I hadn't been introduced to this child and instinct told me to keep it all quite formal.

'Hi,' I said. 'I'm Jo.' Then, nodding at Mabel, added, 'Isn't she lovely?'

'Yeah, she's cute,' he replied.

Matilda had curled up on the sofa beside George, which left me not knowing what to do.

'Well, I've just been speaking to Ian,' I said looking at nobody in particular. 'He's determined that Mabel doesn't stay here. We are going to have to think of something.'

George looked at me and smirked.

'She doesn't bark that much any more and I cover her with my coat when I walk in and out, so Ian has no idea when she is in here. Besides, I've told him she'll be gone in the morning.'

He exchanged a conspiratorial look with his grandson. They both grinned.

Silence. I have no experience of eight-year-old boys, and not knowing if he'd even been told of my existence, I thought it was best that I left.

'See you later, then,' I said, and being careful not to kiss George, I let myself out. Even Matilda had seemed eager for me to go.

I couldn't wait to call Anna to relay all this but the moment I surfaced from the basement flat my phone bleeped to say I had a voicemail. It was Anna.

'Molly's peeing blood again.' She sounded frantic. 'I'm at the vet's round the corner.'

This was what I'd been dreading. The bleeding appeared to have stopped for a few months and, with the help of homeopathy and Rupert To The Rescue, everything seemed to be okay. Now it had returned, proof enough that something was wrong.

I decided to run straight round to the vet's. The voiceover could wait. This was a gamble. Anna is very like myself in that when things go wrong, rather than call out for help, she takes things into her own hands. I'd learned from the episode on the night of the Debbie Harry concert that she wanted to be in control of what was her living nightmare. She didn't want novices fussing around. But I also knew from her leaving me that message that she wanted some support.

She looked up, as white as a sheet, when I arrived in the waiting room. Molly was by her side, shaking like a leaf.

'She hates vets,' Anna said as I sat down next to her, 'but we have to know what's causing this.' I nodded and stroked Molly.

Once again I knew when to shut up. Anna, as well as Molly, despised vets, and would, at any cost, avoid them. However, as she explained to me now, unless the ultrasound revealed exactly where the problem was, she would have nothing to go on.

This veterinary practice was where I took Matilda, and the nurses and receptionist knew me, so when the vet waved Anna and Molly into the surgery, I was allowed to join them. I listened impressed as Anna described vividly her dog's symptoms and asked if she could have a diagnosis with an ultrasound, and then insisted no drugs were to be prescribed. The vet was diplomatic and knew when to respect an owner's request. After briefly examining Molly, he agreed to conduct the ultrasound. He suggested we left her with him for an hour to carry out the tests and perhaps filled in our time 'with a spot of shopping'. How little he knew us. Shopping had never been further from our minds.

'Come on,' I said, grabbing my ashen friend. 'Let's go and get a drink.'

'Where's Matilda?' asked Anna as we settled down to a Pinot Grigio in my local.

'With George, Mabel and his grandson,' I answered.

She nodded, appearing not to have heard the grandson bit.

'I've left Molly to you in my will,' she said, swigging back her wine.

Where had that come from?

'What?' I exclaimed. 'I can't afford her! The supplements alone would bankrupt me, not to mention the vet's bills.'

Secretly, I was hugely flattered. In Anna's life, there was no higher accolade than being entrusted with her dog's welfare. Also, by insinuating Molly might outlive her, she was being positive over the results of the ultrasound.

'Yes, the vet's bills are running into thousands,' she said. 'Thank heavens for insurance. But the costs of the chiropractor and homeopathy, all the holistic treatments, I have to meet myself.' She paused. 'Do you know, since the bleeding occurred on the night of Debbie Harry, do you know what I need to administer to her daily?'

I shook my head. I reckoned I would be told.

'Haematoma: Erigeron 200, Equisetum Hyemale 30, Thlaspi Bursa 30.' She took a breath and carried on, 'Plus when a bout of bleeding occurs, Cantharis 30 every ten minutes for one hour, or every hour if there's bruising around her ear. Haematoma in her ear: Arnica 30, Hammamelis 30, Lachesis 30, three times daily.'

She hadn't finished. 'To prevent infection, instead of antibiotics, I give Hypericum, Myristica, Hepar Sulphur three times daily.'

Unknown to me, this is what she gave Molly every day to keep her well. Anna has a firm belief that traditional drugs cause as many problems as we are told they cure, and her holistic regime was so far fighting Molly's bladder problem.

'Even the acupuncture is costly,' she admitted. 'Rupert doesn't come cheap.'

I was surprised to hear that. I'd assumed, by the way she and Rupert looked at each other, that she was getting a bit on the side, so to speak. But apparently not.

The result of the ultrasound was waiting for us back at the surgery. There was a thickness around the wall of a part of Molly's bladder. This could mean anything. It certainly wasn't cystitis. It might be cancer or it might not. What was evident was that cells from the bladder were flaking off and being passed as clots in the urine.

'What we do now is wait for a few months,' said the vet. 'Then we take another ultrasound to see if it heals or gets thicker.'

Anna held it together. As we left the surgery, Molly trotting by her side, she had the expression of a woman on a mission.

'I'm ordering a giant tub of royal jelly from Norfolk,' she told me. 'Molly will be seeing Rupert for acupuncture twice a week and I'm upping the homeopathy.' I ran to keep up with her.

'Royal jelly is £40 for a week's supply,' I said meanly.

'Too bad,' came the response. 'Nobody is ever shoving drugs into my dog and from now on Molly comes first.'

I hardly dared argue with Anna. This was the right attitude, one of positivity, but as for Molly coming first, it had always been thus.

As on the previous occasion, Molly's bladder problem went into remission, undoubtedly helped by Anna's informed holistic approach. This was a huge relief, not only for Anna and Molly but also for all the people relying on us. We made huge demands of our dogs with appearances and filming and radio studios. If the dogs weren't with us at all these events, fans felt let down.

Anna was adamant, though, that as long as the dogs were healthy and never compromised, all these activities were good for them. She was determined that Molly would not be treated as an invalid. She would administer the best possible holistic care at home, but at the same time, Molly was expected to attend every function and event with the rest of us. This, she was convinced, would help Molly to fight any disease.

With all the concern surrounding Molly's bladder, I had never questioned George over the visit from his grandson. The opportunity had passed.

A few nights after George's grandson and I had met, I finished my show and, as usual, went down to my car, parked outside the BBC. In the lamplight I could make out the two heads of Mabel and Matilda peering over the steering wheel. George had dropped them off a few minutes earlier and they were both eagerly anticipating my arrival. This will always be one of my fondest memories.

Unlocking the car, I nudged them over to the passenger seat and sat myself behind the wheel. Matilda remained where she was, and Mabel did her customary crawl back onto my seat, so that I drove home in the way I had once criticized George for, with her loose on my lap. She sat like a little monkey, looking straight ahead at the headlights from the oncoming traffic, and I prayed no police cars would pick out her profile.

The journey home was only a few minutes and as we stopped at traffic lights in Harley Street, I nuzzled my nose into her little red, furry head, and recoiled. Instead of the lovely warm smell of puppy, a pungent scent of perfume hit me. I drove the rest of the journey avoiding contact with Mabel's head. Pulling over to park outside my block, I leant over to attach Matilda's lead to her collar. The same sharp smell of perfume hit my nose. Where had the two of them been?

I knew George would often sit outside Bar Italia with both dogs and lap up the attention from dancers and actresses on the way into or out of the adjacent stage doors, but they were coated in perfume, as though they had spent hours immersed in it.

Again I was determined to ask George about it but again circumstances prevented me. When he arrived early that morning to collect Mabel, I was fast asleep and didn't hear them leave. My alarm woke me and I leapt straight out of bed, remembering I needed to get a move on. The first London Pet Show was to be launched at Earls Court that weekend, and Anna and I had been invited to open it. This was a big deal for us and we'd been asked to attend a meeting that morning to finalize a running order. But as I mashed raw tripe into Matilda's bowl, a text arrived from Anna: MEETING CANCELLED. THEY RECKON THEY CAN TRUST US TO KNOW WHAT TO DO. ENJOY A FREE DAY X

What a novelty! There I was, wide awake on a weekday morning with the whole day ahead to do what I felt like. I called George.

'Fancy a walk?' I asked. 'I've got the day off.'

'Yippee!' he shouted. 'Let's head to Primrose Hill. I need to get Mabel a harness, she's too fast for a lead. We can go to the pet shop there. I'll be outside in the Skoda in five.'

That's all it took to make him happy.

By the time I'd grabbed Matilda and got downstairs, he was leaning out of the car window – Raybans on, hair out of its usual pony tail – waiting for me.

It had been a while since I'd travelled in his boat of a car and in that time it appeared to have become Mabel's travelling home. Somewhere he had acquired an old plastic dog bed, which he'd stuffed with his discarded sweaters. This was placed on the passenger seat beside him. Mabel sat in the middle. Surrounding her, in the bed, were her toys and snacks. No seat belt in sight.

Obviously, this was how the two of them now travelled. If I'd thought about it, I'd have realized they must have covered a few miles in order for her to need a bed. But nearly everything George did was questionable and I had learned just to accept things.

Matilda and I got into the back and we sped off to Primrose Hill. For George to buy his dog an accessory was very rare. If he could have got away with it, he would have used a bit of old rope as a lead. Mabel's handmade leather collar, designed to match Matilda's, was a gift from me, and although George loved it, he would never spend money on such fripperies. But on this day he was adamant that she should have a harness.

'She's such a gladiator,' he told the pet-shop assistant. 'Man, she pulls so hard the collar is almost choking her. I've been told that a harness would be better.'

While he sorted through harnesses, Mabel sat on the floor, gazing up at him, following his every move. She was still tiny, and her furrowed brow gave her a quizzical expression. Matilda, meanwhile, was scavenging behind the counter.

'I like the red one best,' I said, always determined to take control.

'We'll have the red one,' George told the assistant. 'And let's put it on her now.'

It was May and a beautiful spring morning. The four of us set off up Primrose Hill to its highest point. Mabel, although still very young, and wearing her new red harness, kept up with Matilda as they gambolled ahead. We laughed at their antics. Being bulldogs, they barged and rammed each other and then galloped across the grass sideways. Other walkers we passed, on their way up the hill, stopped to comment on the two of them. That day, they seemed to be making all of Primrose Hill happy.

George and I held the most honest conversation we had ever had with each other on that walk. Neither of us knew then the significance of the moment. Maybe it was the sunshine or the sight of our dogs having fun, but for those couple of hours, everything seemed okay.

'I felt strange meeting your grandson,' I said as we neared the top.

'Yes, that must have been difficult for you,' he answered.

We stopped to get our breath, and looked out over London. This has to be the best-ever view of the metropolis.

'The Post Office tower looks even nearer from here,' George said. 'I took my grandson up there last week.'

Five years it had taken for either of us to mention his grandson in front of one another, and now we had both done so in one morning.

'I might go away with Mabel for a few days,' said George. We had started to go back down the hill towards the Regents Park Gate. The dogs were tumbling around, yards away.

'Where?' I asked, surprised.

'Maybe Hastings,' he said. 'I want to show her the sea.'

'When?' I asked, thinking I would love to see Matilda with Mabel jumping waves.

'Probably this weekend,' he replied.

Then, with a roar, he opened his arms and ran down the hill, towards the dogs. He looked like a birdman about to take flight, with his long grey hair streaming out behind. The dogs ran to meet him, jumping up and down in excitement.

There was no follow-up question about whether I would be free or not. It would have been unnecessary. I was never free at the weekend, especially this one, with the London Pet Show.

I roared down the hill after him and he picked me up and whizzed me around like he'd always done, and then we sat for a while on the grass. He lay back, face up to the sun, and Mabel tucked her body into the crook of his arm. Matilda slotted herself between us, and George fell asleep. He must have been tired. We remained like that, in the sun, for almost an hour and then walked hand in hand back to the Skoda. It was to be the last day we walked the dogs together.

That Friday night, George called me.

'Where are you?' he shouted. I could hear that he was outdoors.

'In the car,' I answered. 'Where are you?'

'Hastings,' he said. Then I heard him say, 'Mabel, here, come here.'

'Are you having fun?' I asked, surprised that he had actually stuck to his plan.

'It's all right,' he answered. Then, the inevitable. 'Don't suppose you're free to come down here?'

I took a deep breath.

'George, I'm doing my breakfast show tomorrow morning, then Anna and I are opening the show at Earls Court. I really can't get away,' I said.

'I'm watching Mabel on the pebbles,' he said. 'Give you an alarm call in the morning.' Then he rang off.

Saturday morning at 5 a.m. and no alarm call. Luckily, my own body clock woke me up. I was cross more than concerned. I sent him a text: WHAT'S UP? IN FIVE YEARS YOU'VE NEVER MISSED MY SATURDAY ALARM CALL. SHOULD I READ ANYTHING INTO THIS?

Then I went in to the BBC and did my breakfast show until 10 a.m. Stopping only to collect Matilda, I headed west to Earls Court to meet Anna. We'd been booked to open the show at 11 a.m. I spotted Anna and Molly in the car park.

'How is she?' I asked, patting a very robust-looking Molly.

'Fingers crossed, okay,' Anna replied. 'I have her on super strength everything at the moment. She's eaten more Royal Jelly than the bloody queen bee.'

We compared outfits. Wrap-around dresses had proved hazardous, so we had settled on colored skinny jeans with leather jackets.

By now, we had opened or judged so many dog shows that we had it down to a fine art. This one was important because it was at Earls Court but the format would be the same. I was becoming accustomed to exhibition halls. After the awe-inspiring NEC, we had worked at Olympia and now Earls Court.

'Right,' said Anna. 'Let's keep things moving. We go into the press office. Shake hands. Get the list of people to thank, make the speech, shout "Woof! Woof!" and keep smiling because a production company will be filming us.'

'Lead the way,' I said, looking at my phone. Still no text from George.

Our loyal band of followers were there to greet us, and they encouraged the rest of the crowd to shout 'Woof! Woof!' at the appropriate moment. We declared the show open. Molly and Matilda stood calmly by our side for the obligatory photographs, then Anna and I shook a lot of hands.

By now, it was mid-afternoon and we were ravenous. We decided to take the dogs outside for a pee and instead of eating in one of the outlets in the cavernous hall, we opted to cross the road and sample one of the cafés near the tube station.

We had just walked out of the VIP gate when I clocked an A-list celebrity, leaning against the wall having a fag. This was an actor with an impressive list of film credits under his belt, as well as many female conquests. I nudged Anna, who on seeing him, looked well chuffed.

'Should I ask him to give us a few words about dogs?' I suggested.

Anna looked doubtful. We often recorded short clips on our phones if we met someone famous, and then played them on the radio show. It tarted up a running order and most celebrities loved the chance to enthuse about their dogs. Up until this moment, nobody had ever declined, which had made us confident enough to approach anyone. This guy was huddled into the wall. I should have guessed from his body language that he wasn't going to oblige. But I waded in regardless.

'Excuse me,' I said, holding out my phone. 'Sorry to bother you. I'm Jo Good from BBC London and I'm wondering, as you're outside a pet show, if you have any thoughts about dogs?'

He turned a look of pure and utter hatred on me. I froze, anticipating what was to come.

'Why don't you people just piss off,' he snarled, 'and bloody well leave me alone.'

I was flabbergasted. I looked at Molly and Matilda for protection. They were standing bored and did nothing. Matilda yawned. Anna grabbed my arm.

'Come on, Jo,' she said, trying to pull me away. 'He's a grump, let's go and have a waffle.'

But I couldn't move. I was incensed at his rudeness and took a step nearer to him. By now he had turned back towards the wall.

'Just let me tell you this,' I said, and he turned back to face me. 'One day you will be grateful for someone like me to plague you, because one day, mate, you will realize that they forget you as quickly as they recognize you, so don't be so bloody rude.'

Still shaking, I allowed Anna to guide me and the dogs across the Earls Court Road to the café opposite.

'What got into you?' she asked after we'd ordered cappuccinos. 'You turned into the she devil.'

'I don't know,' I confessed. 'Oh God, what have I done? I identified myself to him. If he complains to the BBC, I'm out on my ear.'

'Is something up?' Anna asked. 'You really seem stressed, or is it general exhaustion? I've got some Rescue Remedy in my bag.'

'George hasn't been in touch all day,' I told her. 'He didn't call to wake me up and he hasn't sent any annoying texts or pictures of his meals.'

Anna considered this.

'Where is he?' she asked. 'Maybe he's with his music mates, recording.'

'Last night he called me from Hastings,' I said. 'But I couldn't hear the sea.'

We ate our waffles in silence, both summing up the day's activities. I realized I'd over-reacted with the actor, but put it down to being the end of a long week.

Matilda and I walked back with Molly and Anna to the car park. We hugged each other goodbye and I headed home along the West Way to Marylebone. I'd been in the flat just a few minutes when a text arrived on my phone. My heart lifted. This had to be from George. It wasn't. It was from my boss: PLEASE CALL ME ASAP.

The boss never contacted me at weekends. This had to be connected to my outburst with the actor. As I re-read the text, I noticed I had three missed calls. They were all from my boss and must have been made while I was driving home. Oh Lord. I felt sick. I dialled my boss's number. He answered immediately.

'Where are you?' he asked.

'At home,' I answered.

'Is anyone with you?'

'Just Matilda,' I said, beginning to panic.

A pause.

'Jo, I need to come and see you. Can we meet for a coffee?'

I froze.

'What? Why? Oh God, tell me what's happened!'

'I just need to speak to you about something important.'

'Tell me, please tell me. It's George isn't it?' I asked, feeling my knees begin to buckle.

'I'd prefer to meet...'

'Tell me!' I screamed.

I heard him clear his throat and then he said, 'George died early this morning.'

CHAPTER 7

'... a form of morphic resonance.'

'Hiya,' Anna answered the phone. 'I'm cooking sausages.'

'Anna,' I said. 'George has died.'

There was silence. Then an almost inaudible, 'What?'

I heard her sit on the floor. I couldn't say any more. The words wouldn't come out. Only noises.

'I'm on my way, Jo, I'm going to be there very soon. Put the phone down and then I'll almost be there.'

I remember thinking, 'Anna, turn the sausages off. Don't leave the sausages on the stove.'

I waited on my platform bed, Matilda tucked by my side, and concentrated on what little information I'd been told. George had suffered a massive heart attack and died at 4.30 in the morning, with Mabel next to him. On his wife's kitchen floor.

'That doesn't make sense,' said Anna. She had closed all my windows, for fear of Molly jumping out, and was trying to encourage me to drink some alcohol. 'You told me he was in Hastings.'

'None of it makes sense,' I answered, tipping the wine down my throat and morbidly considering whether, if Molly jumped, I would follow.

We sat in silence, caught up in our own thoughts. I couldn't get drunk. If I'd finished the bottle, I would still have been sober.

Simply having Anna there helped. Both dogs were like statues, staring at us. Neither attempted to lie down or relax. It was as if they were on guard, awaiting our orders, sensitive to our traumatised behaviour.

I knew I needed to call several people but the only person I wanted to speak to, at that moment, was his wife. What was he doing there? Was she with him? So many questions, and only she knew the answers, but now was certainly not the time.

Anna and Molly stayed with me through the night. Nobody slept but the four of us huddled together and I remember going up on the roof as it got light, so that Anna could have a cigarette. As the dawn rose on another Sunday in London, I walked to the edge of the terrace and looked out. There was the BT Tower, over-looking George's apartment block, just a four-minute walk away, and there was the roof of the BBC. Every landmark within my sight was connected to George.

The only comfort, during the shock of those first painful days, was my belief that soon I would see Mabel. His wife and his children and grandchildren all had each other, along with a house full of his possessions, but very soon I would be reunited with Mabel. She would return to London, where she belonged.

Practical decisions were being made for me. And for once, I was grateful. I was told that I was to take as much time off from my radio show as I wanted and to return only when I felt ready.

Big George had been the voice of overnight radio in London. Many of the cabbies would listen to me and then stick with him through the early hours. Once off air, he would occasionally join them in one of their green huts for an early breakfast. Many of them had his phone number. They considered him to be their mate and his show had become a sounding board for all their gripes. It was guaranteed that if you took a London cab in the early hours of the morning, almost certainly the driver would be listening, or calling in, to Big George. Before the radio station had released a formal statement, word of his death had spread through their community within minutes. The more vocal drivers called the station and poured out their raw emotions to whichever presenter happened to be on air. They had lost their pal.

At 2 a.m., three days after his death, at precisely the time he would normally have gone on air, a vigil for George was planned by as many London cabbies as could make it. Between them, they sent out the word to gather on the steps of All Souls Church, directly outside the BBC in Portland Place, where they would each hold a candle to their friend. Any drivers who couldn't get there, who maybe had fares in other parts of the city, would acknowledge the moment by turning their lights out and pulling over.

John the Cabbie, one of the most vocal drivers, who was instrumental in getting the message out, had been in touch with me as well as the BBC and hinted that the guys would understand if I declined, but they would appreciate seeing me. I wasn't sure if I was capable of joining them. Anna suggested I should do it for the cabbies, and said that she and Molly would accompany me and Matilda.

I'd already decided that I couldn't attend the family funeral in his home town in the Midlands because it was not my place. I'd never set foot there and the whole town was expected to turn out for the procession. Matilda and me turning up would have been unfair on the family. However, in London, the vigil with the cabbies would be as poignant for me as it was for them.

So, at just before 2 a.m. on the appointed morning, Anna, Molly, Matilda and I walked the familiar route from my apartment, past George's block, to the BBC. He and I had walked that path hundreds of times, but now those same streets were silent and abandoned. That was until we turned the corner into Portland Place.

'Oh gosh,' said Anna, holding my arm. 'I don't believe it.'

Queues of black cabs, all with their lights off, lined either side of the road leading to Oxford Circus. All without drivers. I breathed as deeply as I could, held Anna's hand and clutched Matilda's lead. Ahead of us we could make out a collection of lights bobbing around the shadow of the church. As we got closer, we saw that they were candles, held by hundreds of cabbies, who were wedged together and standing on every step of the church. More were arriving so that they were overflowing into the road.

When they spotted the four of us, the whole crowd engulfed us, patted the dogs, and we were absorbed into their circle. A couple of lady cab drivers had made me a posy of lavender; Rescue Remedy was handed to Anna. John the Cabbie stepped forward.

'I would like us all to join in and sing one of Big George's favourite songs. A song written by a man I knew nothing about until the big fella described his life to me. His name was Louis Armstrong and the song's *What a Wonderful World.*'

As though we had all rehearsed it, we began to sing as loudly as we could. George and I had visited Louis Armstrong's house in New York and George had explained to me how he'd fallen in love with the music as a child. He knew nearly every detail of Armstrong's life and the benevolence of the man. Seldom a night went by when he didn't play an Armstrong track on the show.

I looked at Anna with Molly and at all the drivers singing with such emotion in the cold night air. One of our BBC reporters was standing among them, holding out a microphone so that the vigil could be broadcast live to all the listeners on what would have been George's show. It seemed, for that moment, most of London was mourning.

John the Cabbie drove us back to the flat just as it was beginning to get light. He was clearly shocked by Geoge's death and wanted to know more. As a confidant of George's, I trusted him but I was unable to answer any of his questions. Had he been feeling ill? Was a doctor involved? Where is Mabel? Did I know he was at his wife's? I could only shake my head.

'John, I don't know, I really don't. He'd lost weight, but he'd boasted about it. He told me he was in Hastings.'

As we climbed from the back of the cab, John lent out of his window to tell me something else I didn't know before.

'He overtook me once, on the M1, in the Skoda, late at night, a while back,' he said. 'He was doing a ton. I sent him a text: MATE, CARRY ON LIKE THAT YOU'LL REACH HEAVEN BEFORE ME.'

He laughed at the memory and we looked at each other, probably thinking the same thing. George must have been heading home.

I took just the week off. And that was out of respect for George. I would have preferred to continue doing my show. The building, the studio and the listeners were where I felt safe. It was where George and I had met and it was our world. I knew from the producer that the listeners were in shock and wanted to talk about him on air and I needed to talk to them. Instead, I was on my own, and had nobody to grieve with.

None of his family contacted me. Ian, his caretaker, called me to say that his sons were driving down with a van to clear out his flat, and so I should retrieve anything I wanted quickly, before they arrived.

'Ian, I could never set foot in there,' I said. 'I really couldn't. It would destroy me.'

Ian didn't reply. He was ex-army and not one to display emotion, but just before I hung up, he asked, 'Is Mabel with you?'

'No,' I answered.

I thought maybe his sons would try to contact me while they were in London, since some stuff in the flat was quite obviously mine, clothes for instance. But I heard nothing. Maybe they didn't know if they should, out of loyalty to their mother. Did they see me as friend or foe? What had George actually told his sons?

The only member of his family I'd met was his grandson when I'd turned up at the flat unexpectedly, and that was a fleeting exchange. Had the boy told his parents? Had George explained who I was?

Part of me kept thinking one of them would feel the need to speak to me. Although I had no intention of attending the funeral, surely they would want to know if I would be there, if only to have one less thing to worry about. If, as George had convinced me, the family were okay with our situation, perhaps one compassionate member would call to see how I was doing. Or were they too involved in trying to deal with their own grief?

When I thought along these lines, negativity crept in and I had to stop myself. In the past five years, they had seen very little of him whereas I, apart from the trip to Paris, had seen him every single day. We shared two dogs, we lived in the same street, we worked from the same chair, in the same studio. Every step I took was through George's and my territory. And now I was without him.

His death was so final. It left me not only in emotional pain but with no answers. On the last morning of his life was he happy? Did he speak of me? And even more indulgently, I couldn't stop myself from wondering did he call for me or Matilda when he was in pain? I was so determined not to be drawn into the clichéd scenario of 'them' and me. But their silence was intolerable.

Who had his phone? Was anyone looking at the hundreds of pictures of me with Matilda? Was anyone bold enough to read all the texts, including the final one from me asking why he'd not woken me on that Saturday morning?

I decided to dial his mobile while I was out with Matilda in Hyde Park, not having the courage to risk the familiar territory of Regent's Park. We were limited as to where we could walk because most areas were full of memories of George. Hyde Park had pockets of unexplored corners and if we avoided the statue of Achilles, where the two of us once had a row over ice cream, I was on safer ground.

Crossing Oxford Street, Matilda and I had been recognized by a couple of cabbies. This happened a lot but gone now was the cheeky 'Woof! Woof!' from out of the window.

'Bless you, Jo,' one driver called as he moved off down Oxford Street with a fare in the back. 'Look after that beautiful dog.'

The moment we entered the park I took out my phone and pressed George's name. It went straight to his familiar voicemail, as I knew it would. His great big bugle voice burst out, 'This is Big George! I'm busy!' It had been his idea of a joke.

The bleep went in preparation for my message. I waited, not knowing who, if anyone, was retrieving messages, before quietly saying, 'George ... oh ... George.' There was silence until it disconnected itself.

During my short absence, Anna presented *Barking at the Moon* without me. She had to be bullied into doing so because she always doubts her ability. The irony is that Anna is far more qualified and informed than I am, so when she's confronted with listeners' questions, whether about behaviour or breeding issues, she can deliver a far quicker answer than I can.

On this occasion, however, she was the bridge between the listeners and me. They wanted to know so much but I wasn't there to talk to them. She and the producer knew that all the calls would be about George, Matilda or me and so they cleverly made it easier on themselves by inviting Anne Marie, both Mabel's and Matilda's breeder, on to the show. Unaccustomed to speaking on the radio, she nervously answered Anna's questions with compassion and warmth. Matilda and I were listening at home and I smiled at Anne Marie's description of George in her house in Leicester the day he attempted to choose a pup.

'He loved cake,' she told Anna and the listeners. 'The moment he called me to say he would be coming up I would always say to my daughters, "Bake a cake. Big George is on his way." He adored a moist orange-flavoured sponge.'

'Was Mabel his obvious choice of pup?' asked Anna.

'He made me film the entire litter on his phone,' she replied. 'He picked up each of them in turn, held each one to the camera and said, "Here you go, Joanne. What do you think of this one?"'

Anne Marie was right. I still have the video, on my old phone, of George holding five-week-old Mabel up to the lens, in Anne Marie's home, and asking, 'What do you think, Joanne? Isn't she a cracker?'

He never called me Jo because he said he liked to spend longer on my name. I'd told him not to be so wet.

Rupert to the Rescue, I'd noticed, was seeing more and more of Molly during this time. In other words, he was round at Anna's most days. As she'd watched my world all but fall apart, it seemed to create in her a desire to seek out holistic as well as psychic answers. Maybe she thought it would comfort me.

'Did you spot anything strange in Matilda's behaviour in the lead-up to George's death?' she asked me one evening when I was visiting. My days were spent walking Matilda aimlessly about, avoiding conversations with neighbours, so I'd taken to dropping in for comfort chats.

Rupert was sticking needles into a supine Molly, who lay on a faux fur rug. A strong smell of scented candle mixed with the aroma of spaghetti bolognaise. I'd walked in on a cosy, domestic Saturday night, the first I'd ever witnessed in this part of Islington.

'No, not at all,' I answered. 'Compared with Molly, Matilda isn't the most alert of dogs. She has her likes and her dislikes but life is pretty much all about her next meal.'

Rupert and Anna shared a look. I noticed what looked like a pair of bloke's moccasins by the side of the sofa.

'You always underestimate Matilda's intelligence,' Anna said, kindly. 'Rupert and I have been doing a lot of reading about psychic phenomena in dogs.'

Rupert was placing the final needles into a very calm Molly's head and he nodded in agreement with Anna.

'A lot of paranormal scientists believe in the sixth sense in dogs,' he said. 'It gives them a strong means of communication by thought, which can alert them and us to possible dangers.'

I looked at Matilda now fast asleep on the floor with one of the hooves stuck on her nose, like a comatosed rhinoceros. A bit of a poor relation. It reminded me of her meagre luggage compared with Molly's on the trip to Paris. While Molly languished in laps and bathed in alternative therapies, Matilda was expected to get on with it. I'd learned that from George.

'She's a dog,' he'd insisted. 'She's hardier than you think.'

Anna went to sit beside Rupert, and they both looked at me, presenting a united front.

'This sense is really a natural instinct or telepathic ability that wolves in the wild use all the time,' she said.

Matilda blew off and we all pretended we didn't hear.

'Do you mean Matilda could have been alerting George just prior to his heart attack?' I asked doubtfully. Neither of them answered. 'Well, she would've had a hell of a job,' I said. 'George had no time for psychic phenomena. He laughed at it.'

Rupert nodded. 'Most people do, but some areas are still open for discussion. How, for example, does a dog know when its owner is about to return home?'

'Even if it's at a different time each day,' jumped in Anna.

Rupert was now slipping off his shoes and putting on the moccasins. Did he always keep them there?

'We're not as good as dogs at reading signs, even though we're supposed to be the superior species,' he said. 'Dogs just use their sensory skills. They have an ability to tune in to their owners via a form of morphic resonance – an energetic level.'

Anna has always been intrigued by the psychic connection between humans and dogs, and her bookcase bore witness to this. Now, it seemed, she had a fellow enthusiast in Rupert.

I was sceptical. Nothing in my memory indicated Matilda behaving any differently just prior to George's death. Did Mabel,

I wondered? All I could recall was her right eye constantly running with tears. We had become concerned because George's solution to nearly everything, salt water, hadn't managed to heal it. He had booked an appointment with our vet to have the eye checked at the same time as having her spayed.

Matilda had had this op before her first season, which kept her small, and George had insisted on doing the same with Mabel. This was the only vet's appointment that he had ever made, unlike me, and, being the Tuesday following his death, he never kept it.

Of course, I thought, the vet! He would be able to tell me how Mabel was. That's if the family had knowledge of the operation. He has all of her notes and they would have needed to contact him. I was grasping at straws but any information would be of some comfort.

Unfortunately, the vet's receptionist couldn't offer much help. She knew me well and commiserated over the situation but all she could tell me was that George's wife had called the surgery and asked that Mabel's notes be forwarded to a vet in Milton Keynes.

'Did she sound like she would get the ball rolling?' I asked.

What I really wanted to know, but obviously couldn't ask, was, 'Does she sound nice? Did she mention me? Did she ask about Mabel's co-owner?' Professional etiquette, however, prevented me from probing, so all that my call to the vet achieved was to make me even more determined to speak to George's wife myself.

Only Anna could understand why. Without exception, all other friends and colleagues urged me not to contact her, and asked the same question – 'Why? What will you achieve?' If it hadn't been for Mabel, maybe I never would have.

But while one family comforted, supported and grieved together in the Midlands, my little London family was fragmented. For me, my family had been George and 'his girls', and the youngest of those was now separated from us. I was pining for her. My shambolic George had taught me to love and nurture from the moment he found Matilda. Until then, I had never looked after, or wanted to mother, anything. I would often joke that I was born without any maternal instincts. I lived a single, career-driven life, cleverly avoiding any responsibilities, so that all I worried about was ME.

However, that began to change from the time George moved in and culminated in total devotion with the introduction of Matilda. Together we built around us a tiny but loving home, complete with baby gate, toys, sleepless nights and all that a puppy involved. As she grew, so did my love for her. We were a unit, with Matilda always our prime concern.

George, unintentionally, had guided me through a process of parenting, delivering invaluable lessons, such as getting her only ever to pee in the kerb, never on the pavement. He explained how trigger words, introduced as a puppy, meant she would relieve herself on command. Still, to this day, it's one of her most impressive traits. He calmly disciplined her to be patient, so that when

I burst out of my yoga class on to Oxford Street, they would be waiting outside, big man standing and little dog sitting nicely by his side. Matilda's wonderful and often-described loving nature came from George and was continued through me.

With Mabel, the process had been repeated. She burst into our lives with all her energy and barking, like a naughty little sister. This time, an older dog was there to help train her, and Matilda, somewhat grudgingly, took to the role. Now, when we uttered the trigger words, the two of them would squat on command.

The sheer geography of Mabel living down one end of the street but sleeping every night on my bed kept George's and my relationship going. At a time when I was working long hours, the choreography required to keep Mabel with one of us at all times to prevent George from being evicted meant we actually saw more of each other. George would wait for me, outside my yoga class or the supermarket, with both dogs sitting side by side, wearing their bow-tie collars (my influence), in decreasing size, like a pair of Russian dolls. My family.

Mabel, like Matilda, had taken her first steps as a puppy on the streets of London. Soho, and Bar Italia, was her afternoon outing, the Honest Sausage in Regent's Park the weekly treat, the scent around her neck was George's Jo Malone and her sleeping place was my platform bed. We were a loving, if somewhat dysfunctional, family, but now one member of that family had gone and another was missing. It was time to bring her home.

The decision was prompted by an email I had received from Anne Marie, who had attended George's funeral. She had told the family of Mabel's need to be spayed and the concern over her eye, and she wanted to tell me that Mabel had been in attendance on the day. Apparently, George's wife had sat her on her lap throughout the service and she had behaved impeccably, not moving, but staring straight at the chaplain.

The email was sent with affection and I suppose was intended to help, but the feelings that image of his wife conjured up in me were indescribable. I understood completely why she would want to hold on to George's dog, and hug her close, because I did too. In my mind, Mabel was the closest I could get to smelling or touching George. And I hadn't seen either of them since the day we bought her red harness in Primrose Hill.

For days I tried to pluck up courage to pick up the phone. How would I start the conversation? How would I introduce myself? What did this woman know about me?

The *Guardian* had been asked to reprint their obituary. In the first version, they had stated, 'George is survived by his partner, broadcaster Jo Good.' This was altered in the second version, printed the next day, to, 'George is survived by his wife and children and grandchildren' etc. And that's as it should have been. I agreed, when I read it, that it should have been amended.

Eventually, I made the phone call to her from the privacy of George's and my studio, at work. I timed it for 30 minutes before my show was due to go to air. That way I had a reason to pull myself together, whatever the result might be. In the studio the lights are low and it's sound-proofed. All kinds of things may be going on on the other side of the glass, but I'm distanced from them. It's where I feel safest. Also, importantly and unlike my flat, it's anonymous.

I dialled the landline number and waited. In my mind, I was picturing where the phone might be. A country kitchen? The room where he collapsed? Was she at home? Maybe it would be a son who answered.

Eventually, the phone was picked up and I knew that the voice on the other end was that of his wife.

As a journalist and presenter, I am expected to visualize what I want out of an interview and to stick to the questions in order to achieve it. In this instance, I failed. I felt my faltering conversation with Sheila was the most awkward and frustrating of any I had ever experienced in that studio.

I had wanted answers to three things:

Had George really left her?

Did she know about me and therefore want to ask me about George's life in London?

Could I bring Mabel home?

She was very hesitant. There were more silences than there were words, and it seemed that she didn't want to talk to me. I gently attempted to coerce her into conversation by playing down my relationship with George and encouraging her to speak about hers.

I waited patiently through every silence.

On the other side of the glass I could see Tony Blackburn joking with his producer. What on earth would any of them have made of this? Everybody had warned me against it.

When eventually she started to open up, it was as though she was almost talking to a stranger enquiring about her husband's death.

I had trouble following the conversation as she began to talk about the practicalities of coping with the situation; the company and his office in Marylebone; the closeness of the family during this period; how she and George first met...

As her memories came flooding out, I agreed with her on every point, thinking that this was the only way I would find my answers.

There was no indication that she had been awaiting or dreading my call. I'd wanted her to meet me half way, but she didn't ask one question and this both mortified and frustrated me to such an extent that I started to silently weep.

Tears dripped onto the desk as she pressed on, telling me what a comfort to her Mabel had become and how she had never realized how much work it was to rear a bulldog.

Again, I agreed. I knew that I would never ask if I could bring Mabel home.

So, instead, I bravely suggested I might come up and visit Mabel, as I'd not set eyes on her since the day before George's death.

She explained that that would not be possible and the conversation ended.

For a long time I sat in the semi darkness of the studio, watching the mayhem of the radio station outside, playing it all over again in my mind. Soon my producer would walk in, so I should pull myself together.

What had I hoped to achieve from that phone call? I knew the answer. It was deluded but simple – a date when I could collect Mabel, and maybe an invitation to sit and talk about George's final years in London. How naïve.

From the moment she had answered I realized that none of that would be possible. To even suggest that I bring Mabel back to London would have been ridiculous as well as insensitive. It was obvious from our short conversation that I wasn't even on her radar, and what was more alarming, she spoke as though he had always lived there. His flat was referred to as his London office because they ran a company. Doing what?

George had actually told me early on in the relationship that he had signed over everything to the family so that he could live independently in London. 'You set me free,' he said to me. That comment, along with his insistence that the family were 'cool about everything' had always convinced me that I should feel no guilt. Had I refused to see what was in front of my very eyes?

Now, as I prepared to go on air, I played the conversation back in my mind and 'cool' was not the way I would have described his wife's tone. Had he lied to me? What had he been up to? Was he playing us all along, just to keep the boat from rocking? So as not to upset any of us?

I did my show that night on automatic pilot and I continued to take calls from listeners wanting to talk about George. Many of them were living on their own and lonely, and now struggling to deal with life without him, and so the radio show seemed to be a place of comfort for all of us. None of them, however, could have imagined the soap opera of a scenario his death had left behind.

'You need a long walk,' said Anna the following day. 'Let's take the girls to Kenwood, and let them run.'

I had hinted in a text that I had loads to tell her, and that I was still coming to terms with most of it. Anna, more than anyone else, would understand. She never judged me and had not once questioned my anxiety at being unable to see or hold this small dog.

Hampstead has to be the best-ever place to walk dogs in London. It's why so many films, books and documentaries have been made about the subject. If humans feel a sense of euphoria there, imagine the effect on dogs. It is the highest point in London, so maybe the fresher air or the sense of space have something to do with it, but whatever it is, dogs seem happier and more liberated there. Our two become energized the moment they see Parliament Hill. With not a building in sight, they literally gallop abreast like a pair of greyhounds, then ram and jump over each other. It makes us laugh and call their names, and then they do it again. Hampstead seems to inspire them even more than countryside.

That summer's day conditions were perfect for the Heath – clear blue sky, a slight breeze and enough dogs out for walks to keep them all interested. Aware that I was still mulling stuff over, Anna said nothing for a while but eventually broke into my thoughts.

'Rupert and I are going to The Four Seasons in Hampshire for the weekend,' she told me, as we strolled past the ladies pond. She was wearing denim shorts, a Hendrix T-shirt and a great big grin. 'They offered me a freebie 'cos they're promoting dog-friendly, five-star accommodation, and I said I could help.'

'Isn't that the place you can hire horses?' I asked, pleased for her.

'You bet,' she answered. 'We've already booked a couple of bays for Sunday morning. Rupert loves to ride and has a 14-hander as a client in Richmond. He says his fetlock benefits from weekly acupuncture ... the horse's, that is.'

With all that had been going on in my life, it had slipped my notice how much Anna talked about Rupert. Maybe the recent events had drawn them a bit closer. I'd always assumed, when she mentioned him, it was because of his connection with Molly and his attentiveness to her bladder problem. He was so straight and quaint, compared to Y Bother, and he appeared less complicated. In no way was I dismissing his attractiveness, but the fact that he had managed to set Molly back on the path of good health, at least for the time being, to Anna, would have turned him into the Messiah.

'Anna, I phoned George's wife,' I said.

She kept walking, looking down at the grass, taking it in.

'Right. And what did she say? Are you bringing Mabel back?'

'I'm not certain she knew who I was,' I answered.

Anna stopped and looked at me.

'What? You mean she pretended she didn't know who you were?'

'She didn't make one reference to George's and my relationship,' I continued. 'She spoke to me as though I was a friend enquiring about her wellbeing. She talked about the financial situation they were left in.'

Anna, hands on hips, frowned and chewed her bottom lip. You could read her like an open book.

'What's more,' I continued. 'I don't think he had told any of his friends or family about me.'

Before she could answer, both dogs drew our attention. We were approaching the lake in front of Kenwood. Soon they would be setting out the stage for the summer concerts. Over the summers, George and I had been lucky enough to see Rufus Wainwright and Brian Wilson from the Beach Boys. On that night, we danced ourselves crazy.

The girls, glorying in their freedom, had taken off across the grounds in front of us, towards the stunning house. This was one of the few places where Anna was happy to let Molly off the lead – there were no roads close by and nothing to distract her but glorious open space. Even so, they were disappearing from sight and we knew we should run to keep an eye on them. Galloping over the brow, they resembled stick-like Lowry figures against the grassy background. As we ran towards them, for that moment, all else was forgotten and we felt as energized as our dogs.

Then they both stopped. Anna's antennae went up. Initially, it was difficult to see what had halted them. As we got nearer, we could make out that they were sniffing around something on the grass.

'Bet you somebody has left bits of a picnic behind,' gasped Anna, trying to catch her breath. Always fearful of alien food, she took off again at speed after them. I followed, watching as she joined the dogs and looked down to see what had distracted them. When I finally caught up, she was still staring at the ground.

'Oh Jo,' she said, still puffing, and I followed her gaze.

On a metal manhole cover, set deep in the grass in the centre of Kenwood's massive grounds, painted in large silver letters, were the words:

BIG GEORGE

REAL

R.I.P

I have no idea who wrote that or why in such an obscure location. It would be easy to walk by and not even notice it. Thousands of visitors probably have, but it drew the attention of our dogs. The tribute has endured all weathers. It's still there.

Anna persuaded me to find a table in Kenwood's tea garden and calm down. But I was very calm. She and Rupert had encouraged me to consider our sixth sense, explore the psychic phenomena, but for me this was sign enough. George's presence was everywhere, even here on this beautiful heath where the air was fresh and our dogs ran free.

'I've decided to visit George's wife,' I told Anna. 'I need to see Mabel. You, of all people, must understand how I feel. She's the only bit of him that isn't shrouded in mystery.'

We were tying the dogs to the table leg and, as usual, they had drawn a lot of attention from other owners.

'So is it the wife or Mabel you really want to see?' replied Anna, checking the knot on Molly's lead. 'Because you can't force her to let you in.'

'I'm out on a limb,' I said. 'I'm so confused that I'm beginning to doubt everything that George and I had together. The only thing I trust is Mabel's and my love for one other. I need to experience that and let her know I haven't abandoned her.'

'Of course,' said Anna. 'Besides, she can't slam the door in your face once you're there.'

Just then a loud bang came from under the table as Matilda's head shot up and hit it. The reason for her exuberance was clear. A large bloke, George-like in appearance, was patting and admiring Molly, and Matilda had initially convinced herself that it *was* him.

This happened regularly when large men came within her eyeline. Her behaviour had been affected in many ways, and I had learned to watch for trigger signs. For instance, we never turned left out of my block because that had been the way to George's and it was the direction she always looked towards. So now, even if it meant we took a major detour, we only ever turned right. We also stopped using the name George in front of her. When she was within earshot, he was referred to as BG. It was kinder.

I looked at her now, as the eager bloke bent down and the realization dawned on her that he was a stranger.

'And I'm taking Matilda with me to see Mabel,' I said to Anna.

'Then Molly and I are coming too,' she said. 'We love a day in the country.'

It was wet and windy on the day we made that journey up the M1. The girls were in their customary position on the back seat, although we'd got lazy about strapping them in, so they were free to move about. As I gazed through the windscreen wipers at the passing Buckinghamshire landscape, I imagined George making the same journey, so many times, in his Skoda. Anna was silent, fiddling with the Sat Nav on her phone and probably feeling as unsure as I was whether we were doing the right thing.

I enjoy driving because it's the one time I manage to think without distraction. So now, as we travelled towards George's world, although the fear in my stomach increased as we got closer and closer, I tried to piece things together.

John the Cabbie had seen George on this road, doing a ton, going in the wrong direction, while I was on air. He was obviously heading home. But for how long? This was on a weekday and he had to do a show straight after mine. At weekends, of course, over the summer, we had been filming most days, so George was left to fill his time until late evening, when I'd get back. Except, of course, on the Paris weekend.

'Do you remember when we got back from Paris?' I asked Anna. 'George was still living with me and the bed hadn't been slept in.'

She immediately understood what I was getting at.

'Do you think he'd gone home to his wife?' she asked.

'I think all the time Matilda and I were busy working, or when I was on air, he would pop up there,' I said. 'I don't believe he would ever take Matilda.'

I thought of the time I had smelt perfume on Mabel's head but not on Matilda's. Was Mabel, by that time, familiar with George's family? I knew she had played with his grandson but that was only because I had walked in on them.

I kept staring at the road ahead, thinking about George being with his family.

'I don't think she knew about me.' The thought had kept coming back to me. 'Anna, I don't think he ever really left home.'

'What! You can't be serious! The two of you were everywhere, in newspapers, magazines ... he went on and on about you on the radio ...

She was right. Even if his family didn't read tabloids, surely one of them would have listened to his radio show. Most nights George would start the show totally unprepared and resort to talking about his antics with me and Matilda. He even asked the listeners, on air, how he could persuade me to marry him! Although his wife and sons didn't live locally, all of this could be heard on the internet.

Why had none of his family, or his friends, contacted me since his death? Maybe because I'd never met any of his friends, apart from the artist at Tony's dinner party that is. George had shown no sign of recognition when we met her, hadn't introduced me, and yet at the end of the evening she told me she was a friend of his and his wife's. It was obviously a discussion he had hoped to avoid. How many occasions had we brushed close by his 'other' life?

Just as we reached the turn-off, Matilda thrust herself on to Anna's lap and sat there stubbornly, pretending to look at the passing scenery. Molly, on the other hand, was already asleep on the floor, under the dashboard, by Anna's feet, her favourite place.

'His village is the next exit,' said Anna, studying the Sat Nav. 'Have you got the address?'

I reached into my jeans' pocket and pulled out an old envelope. On it I'd scribbled the street name I'd copied from an obituary in the local press. I could have asked for the full address from the BBC but they would have questioned it.

'Hang on a minute,' said Anna, looking at the envelope. 'So we have the street but no house number. What do you plan on doing? Knocking on every door and asking if Mabel's in?'

I started to slow down as we entered the outskirts approaching the high street. It was a typical English market town with a couple of pubs and shops either side. Had George drunk in those pubs? Did he buy his newspaper in that newsagent's? This was the street his funeral procession had gone down. I'd seen a clip of it on You Tube, and it seemed the whole town had turned out to lend their support. Big George in this rural setting seemed so unlike the George I knew. This was a million miles away from the diversity and madness of Soho or Bar Italia. What had he done here? Where did he hang out? His home, of course.

'From the name of his street, it's obviously near the canal,' I said.

We had parked up outside one of the pubs. Incredible to think there was no restricted parking. Still not reason enough, I thought, to live in a place like this.

Anna was struggling to read her Sat Nav with Matilda refusing to budge from her lap.

'His street is second on the left,' she said. 'From what I can see, it's opposite that bridge, just by the side of the boathouse.'

I felt absolutely sick with nerves. Was this the right way to go about things?

'Okay, so what do you plan on doing?' Anna asked. 'Walking up and down the street until one of his family see fit to take Mabel out for a walk, then rushing up and introducing yourself? We haven't really thought this through, have we?'

Anna and I walking up and down a tiny riverside path in five-inch heels, wearing leather jackets and leading two bull breeds, would hardly meld into the landscape of the local environment. We would be as obvious as Paul O'Grady in drag.

'You know we could be accused of stalking?' she added.

I kept my eye on passing shoppers. Was one of them his wife? Don't let it be that thin one coming out of the stationer's. Or the blonde crossing the road in front of us.

'Right,' I said slowly. 'I have a plan. We'll turn into his street, park up and wait. At some point somebody will have to take Mabel for a walk and then I'll see her. That's all I want, just to see her. We needn't get out of the car.'

I started the engine and pulled back out into the high street, then took the second left into his road. I could hardly turn the wheel my palms were so clammy.

It was indeed a tiny, narrow street of about ten houses on one side and a stagnant canal on the other. Residents' cars were parked close to hedges so even my tiny mini had to squeeze to get through. What happened next was so sudden that I had no time to react sensibly.

Matilda, who up until now had been seated on Anna's lap, jumped up at the passenger window and, finding it closed, thrust her head on the windscreen, straining to get out of the car.

'Matilda, stop,' screamed Anna and I could see claw marks appearing on her arms as she attempted to hold her down. Matilda's eyes were rolling and she rammed at the closed window again with the full strength of her hard head. Molly, alarmed, tried to jump out of her space from under the seat so that Anna was having to deal with the weight of two dogs.

'Stop the car!' yelled Anna. 'Jo, stop!'

Jamming on the brakes, I reached over to pull on Matilda's collar, trying to stop her injuring herself and it was then that I looked up and saw the trigger for this chaos. Opposite was the Skoda. George's pride and joy. Matilda had seen it from the moment we had turned into his street.

'Turn the car round,' Anna shouted. 'We must get out of here.'

'I can't,' I snapped. 'There's no space. I'll have to reverse.'

'Just be quick,' said Anna from beneath a pile of barking dogs. 'We're drawing so much attention to ourselves.'

Curtains were beginning to twitch as I put my foot down and we hurtled backwards from whence we came. We let the dogs out when we reached the high street. They both stood panting and staring at us, with a look of 'What the hell was that about?' Matilda started to yawn. It was her own attempt to calm things down.

'Give me a cigarette,' I said to Anna.

'No,' she answered, lighting one for herself. 'You gave up ten years ago.'

'This was a ridiculous idea,' I said.

'At least we now know which house it is,' she said, blowing smoke away from my face. 'And that there's an alley running behind it.'

'Is there?' I asked, becoming more interested.

She was right. From where we were standing by the car, we could see a small path leading behind the houses, past all their back gardens. We had got this far so why not? Determined not to set Matilda off again, we put the dogs back in the car and approached the alley.

We knew exactly which one was George's back garden and from the height of the line of back fences, it was obvious we would be able to see straight over it. Every garden had a washing line and in the first house a man was mending a bike. Our two blonde heads would have been just apparent as we approached George's house, and I planned on bobbing down. However, just at that moment, we heard a noise as though the back door was about to open.

This might well have been everything I'd been waiting for – my glimpse of Mabel or the wife or a son. But I couldn't brave it out. I lost my nerve. The moment that back door opened, I freaked out. If Mabel had come skipping out, I knew I could never have walked away from her. Besides, we were virtually trespassing. There was no reason for us to be on this path. If George had ever thought I'd behave in such a way, he would have been horrified.

I ducked down and ran, horizontally, back up the path and could sense that Anna was following me. The whole operation had been a washout. Deep down, I didn't have the nerve to follow it through.

'Let's just go home now,' I said, as we walked back towards the car. 'We have no right to be here.'

I felt so cross with George. Why had he left everything in such a mess? It was his fault, after all, that I'd behaved so irrationally.

Anna glanced over at me before sliding into the passenger seat.

'I'm glad you look out of place,' she said kindly. 'Complexions such as yours don't age well in the country.'

It was important that I accepted I was never going to see Mabel again. Only Anna really understood how much that devastated me.

A few days after the disastrous trip, I collected all of her collars and leads and, along with a bottle of fish oil (essential to bulldogs), stuffed them in a padded envelope and posted them to George's wife with a note: 'Mabel left these behind.'

Soon after that, Anna dropped another bombshell concerning George's death.

'All of the videos George took of us and the girls have been removed from the internet,' she called to tell me one day. 'Only he could have taken them off. Why?'

This was very odd. Those videos had springboarded our success and now the only one left was of George and Matilda on the set of a commercial, which I had shot on his camera. It was Matilda's first professional appearance and George was talking her through it and keeping her calm.

Two other things left me wondering if he knew that he was ill or heading for another heart attack. My mother had received from him, a month prior to his death, a bound album of photographs, mapping our six-year relationship. Holidays in New York and Paris were recorded, along with pictures of the dogs, all in chronological order. She was thrilled, but the gift had been unexpected since the two of them seldom met.

What really baffled me, though, was his locker at work. Each presenter has their own labelled locker, but neither George nor I used them much, and certainly never thought to lock them. When I returned to work after my leave of absence, I suddenly thought to look in his, and opened the door with some trepidation. In it was a pile of assorted CDs, a toothbrush and a massive brown envelope. I held my breath as I tipped it out. Hundreds of photographs fell on to the desk. Every photograph taken of me and Matilda, or the three of us, was there. I recognized them as the ones he had on the walls of his flat because they still had his messages written on them in felt tip. He must have cleared them all out of his flat, but when? I'd been in there just days prior to his death. Had he planned on moving out? Had he foreseen what eventually happened and wanted to spare his family?

'Let it go,' said Anna when she saw how much it was getting to me. 'You have Matilda and maybe one day, when you're ready, you'll get another dog.'

This was something I'd been suggesting to her. Molly was now ten and although, between them, Rupert and Anna were keeping her healthy, the bladder issue was not going away. Never did Molly pee without the two of us examining it for signs of blood – always the relief when it was clear, and always the stress when it wasn't.

Despite Anna's declarations of ending her own life when Molly passed on, I knew that having another dog in the house would ease the pain. But she would have none of it.

'There has only ever been Molly and me in this life,' she said emphatically. 'How could I, in her final years, expect her to share me and the home with another dog? It's the very last thing she needs.'

I understood, and was therefore surprised when the situation was solved by the arrival of a kitten, of all things. It appeared outside her back door, miaowing and staring through the glass.

'But you hate cats,' I said to her. 'What made you take it in?'

'I think of him as a messenger,' said Anna. 'I never intended him to stay. He arrived from nowhere and I've asked around but nobody has claimed him. I've named him Gremlin.'

It was as though he was heaven sent because he brought out the playful side of Molly. Instead of resenting him, she would play rough and tumble, and they became a little family unit, albeit a slightly odd one.

Gremlin enjoyed none of the luxuries with which Molly was indulged. He was turfed out at night, not allowed in the bedroom and never taken to the vet's. Anna's only concession to spoiling him was to feed him raw food, which, in the long run, would actually benefit him. With Rupert, Gremlin and Anna's cocktail of homeopathy, Molly seemed to be living a healthy life.

Barking at the Moon continued to broadcast every Thursday night. Word had got round that the only agenda was the relationship with your dog, so we were managing to entice some groovy guests on to the show, including Mika, Macy Gray and, eventually, Robbie Williams, who tweeted that our radio interview was the best he had ever given. Our guest list was booked for months ahead and Anna, with all her knowledge and expertise, was frequently asked on to *Breakfast News*, as a pundit, to comment on canine stories.

One Thursday we featured an item due to air on BBC 1, a documentary called *Pedigree Dogs Exposed*. It explored the health and welfare issues surrounding pedigree dogs and the habits of breeders. Ironically, the British bulldog, like Matilda, is considered to be one of the controversial breeds with concerns over breathing and birthing. George and I had prided ourselves that in Anne Marie we had found a responsible breeder, who bred healthy dogs, with longer legs and snouts than most. She and other bulldog breeders are attempting to get the head and limbs back to the Victorian bulldog shape.

Pedigree Dogs Exposed caused plenty of comment and reaction, and our listeners were eager for their voices to be heard. Criticism and blame were being hurled all over the place and our Facebook page became very active.

Weeks later, on a non *Barking at the Moon* night, I was on air, playing a track and scrolling through the internet, with just an hour left of taking calls before heading back home. I went on to our Facebook page and somebody had posted a link to *Pedigree Dogs Exposed*. I clicked on to it and it went straight to a message board section. Even before I had a chance to read the messages I saw her. Mabel, in her red harness, the last thing we'd ever bought her, bounced up on my screen. She was running in her customary fashion and looking over her shoulder. Above her was written: ABLE MABEL.

The track was about to finish but I couldn't trust myself to speak, so I fired another one. She was longer and leggier than when I'd last seen her but still with the worried expression and furrowed brow. Underneath somebody had written: 'Isn't this the finest specimen of bulldog you have ever seen, running like a whippet?' Tears were streaming down my face. George would have been so proud of his little girl, looking just as he'd wanted her to.

Somehow I limped through to the end of the show. When I got home, I emailed the documentary's producer, Jemima Harrison. I explained that I had a history with this dog and would be interested to know when and where the photograph was taken. George's wife didn't seem the sort to boast about her pet on a message board.

By the time I woke up the following morning, Jemima had emailed back. She told me that the photograph was taken in a town in the Midlands – George's town – by a friend of hers, who saw Mabel out walking most days. This friend had asked the owner if she could take the photograph because Mabel was such a perfect example of a healthy bulldog. The picture, as I then realized, had been taken in the playing field near George's house.

I haven't seen Mabel other than in that photograph, but just to know that she's fit and hasn't been left, like so many of the breed, to run to fat makes me feel good.

Anna and Molly, Matilda and me – we had bumped along the same rocky old road of highs and lows for so long now that no explanations were necessary any more. Anna knew me so well that on the occasions when we spotted a large man with a small mischievous puppy, our eyes met and we didn't need to say a word. I understood her total devotion to Molly, her 'eccentricity' surrounding her love of her dog, to the point that I could name every one of her homeopathic remedies! In turn, Anna knew when to steer me away from reminiscing and when to allow me to indulge in the George days.

I have always believed that her so-called psychic connection is more apparent between the two of us than evident in our dogs. She'll call to say, 'Come on, let's take the girls for a run,' just when I need to see them. Off we head to the Honest Sausage, discussing ideas and laughing as the girls ram each other. Just an hour of each other's company and we all return home feeling so much better.

In the following months, *Barking at the Moon* went from strength to strength. Then came the news that the station was to be re-launched and my show would move to daytime. My boss was inundated with calls, letters and emails demanding to know if the 'dog show' would continue, which it did, although not without its problems.

Our first daytime show created quite a stir. During the day, the building is heaving with staff and security, giving it a far different feel from at night-time. And of course, daytime broadcasts reach a far larger audience. Molly and Matilda entered the building through the same door the DG had recently walked out of after resigning. They joined journalists and camera crew in the lift and trotted through the open-plan newsroom. Workers left their posts to stroke them and have a chat as word had got round that a doggy radio show was about to air somewhere in the building.

As the opening theme tune by the Jive Aces burst on to the airwaves, Molly joined in the chorus with her usual gusto and I could see from the looks on the faces of the people outside that she had proved the studio wasn't sound proof.

That afternoon an email from the boss dropped into my inbox. In it he said that it was not acceptable to have dogs in the building during the day for Health and Safety reasons. He also mentioned that the sound of Molly's barking could be heard all the way through BBC Persia's news bulletins, on the floor above. He suggested that from now on *Barking at the Moon* would not be able to have dogs in the studio.

I called Anna that night to report the situation to her. She and Rupert were curled up on the sofa with Molly watching *Beverly Hills Chihuahua.*

'Ready to do battle'? I asked.

'Woof! Woof!' came the reply.

Also available from Hamlyn:

TILLY: THE UGLIEST CAT IN THE SHELTER
By Celia Haddon

A heart-warming true story of how an ugly, unwanted, cowering young cat helped her owner through the most difficult time of her life.

Tilly was in an Oxfordshire shelter, unchosen, scared and practically feral, until Celia began a project to transform her into a household pet. Through Tilly's journey from unadoptable cat to adored and adoring pet, Celia embarks on her own inward journey and, as events take a dramatic turn, she comes to realize that she needs Tilly as much as Tilly needs her.

Throughout all the difficulties in Celia's life, cats have played a vital role and they have even saved her from herself. This is a story for all those who've gained solace from their pet. It's an absorbing study of how animals can help you through the hardest of times.

ISBN: 978-0-600-62466-0
Price: £7.99

HELL ON 4 PAWS
By Gwen Bailey

Gwen Bailey is one of the UK's most respected dog behaviour experts. She has helped millions of owners transform their troublesome pets into obedient hounds. So what happened when she met Chesil, one of the most dysfunctional dogs in all her years of experience... and she just so happened to be her new partner's dog?

This is a wonderful and witty tale of how Gwen's life was turned upside-down when she took on a new man, his family and an unruly Chesapeake Bay Retriever, one of her greatest challenges both emotionally and professionally. Not only did she have to adjust to a new life, but she also had to deal with Chesil's crazy antics.

Could Gwen take this unruly beast and turn her into an award-winning hound? Find out in this inspirational tale that will appeal to anyone who's ever felt their dog was untrainable.

ISBN: 978-0-600-62176-8
Price: £7.99

DOG WALKS MAN
By John Zeaman

*'There is a hope that a dog injects into every walk, more than
a hope – an expectation really – that this is going to be something
wonderful. You'll see, says the dog, something great is going to
happen – just you wait.'*

John is an art critic who, like dads the world over, is duped into
getting a dog by his children. Together, he and Pete (a standard
poodle named after a Ghostbuster) discover that the simple dog
walk opens up a whole new world on their doorstep. Day by day,
walk by walk, they journey through their neighbourhood's fringes
discovering its natural wonders and the characters within.

Each chapter is a meditation on a new theme and a new
adventure. Woven into the absorbing narrative are the
timeless issues of how dogs drag you into the most unlikely
of conversations; of dog walkers' envy of those who find mafia
murder victims and the childish joy of finding wild, no rules,
dog-walking land in which you can both feel free. This is a
touching, witty and thought-provoking tale of how one man
found meaning in the humble dog walk.

Available as an e-book only
E-book ISBN: 978-0-600-62329-8
Price: £4.99